D1511410

INVESTIGATING
DISEASES

Investigating
Tuberculosis and Superbugs

Library of Congress Cataloging-in-Publication Data

Kelly, Evelyn B.
 Investigating tuberculosis and superbugs: real facts for real lives /
 Evelyn B. Kelly, Ian Wilker, and Marylou Ambrose.
  p. cm.—(Investigating diseases)
 Summary: "Provides information about tuberculosis and other drug-resistant
 diseases, including treatment, diagnosis, history, medical advances, and true
 stories about people with the diseases"—Provided by publisher.
 Includes bibliographical references and index.
 ISBN 978-0-7660-3343-6
 1. Drug resistance in microorganisms—Juvenile literature. 2. Multidrug-resistant
 tuberculosis—Juvenile literature. I. Wilker, Ian. II. Ambrose, Marylou. III. Title.
 QR177.K45 2011
 616.9'041—dc22

                                                                                    2009037811
Printed in the United States of America

052010 Lake Book Manufacturing, Inc., Melrose Park, IL

10 9 8 7 6 5 4 3 2 1

To Our Readers:
We have done our best to make sure all Internet Addresses in this book were active and
appropriate when we went to press. However, the author and the publisher have no
control over and assume no liability for the material available on those Internet sites
or on other Web sites they may link to. Any comments or suggestions can be sent by
e-mail to comments@enslow.com or to the address on the back cover.

✪ Enslow Publishers, Inc., is committed to printing our books on recycled paper. The
paper in every book contains 10% to 30% post-consumer waste (PCW). The cover board
on the outside of each book contains 100% PCW. Our goal is to do our part to help
young people and the environment too!

Investigating
Tuberculosis and Superbugs
Real Facts for Real Lives

**Evelyn B. Kelly, PhD, Ian Wilker,
and
Marylou Ambrose**

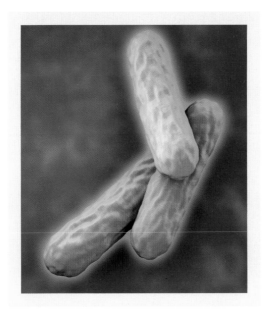

Enslow Publishers, Inc.
40 Industrial Road
Box 398
Berkeley Heights, NJ 07922
USA

Table of Contents

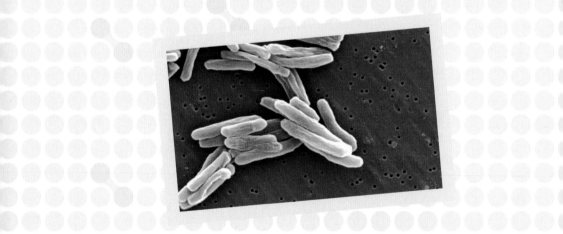

What Are Tuberculosis and Other Superbugs?

WHAT IS TUBERCULOSIS?

Tuberculosis is an infectious, potentially fatal disease that is caused by bacteria and usually affects the lungs. It is commonly referred to as TB.

HOW DO YOU GET IT?

TB is generally difficult to catch. It is contracted by inhaling air that contains droplets contaminated with TB bacteria.

WHAT ARE THE SYMPTOMS?

Symptoms of tuberculosis include fatigue, fever, loss of appetite, weight loss, night sweats, persistent cough, chest pain, and blood in sputum.

HOW IS IT PREVENTED?

Tuberculosis may be prevented by avoiding close contact with people who have active TB, and by staying healthy so the body can fight off infection. A vaccination called BCG helps prevent TB in many parts of the world, but it is not widely effective and not commonly used in the United States.

HOW IS IT TREATED?

TB is treated with drugs called antibiotics, taken over a period of several months to two years. The drugs must be taken exactly as prescribed for the amount of time the doctor orders or drug-resistant strains of TB can arise.

WHAT IS DRUG RESISTANCE?

Some disease-causing organisms mutate so that they are no longer killed by drugs, most often antibiotics. They are referred to as drug-resistant organisms, or superbugs.

HOW MANY OTHER DRUG-RESISTANT DISEASES, OR SUPERBUGS, ARE THERE?

There are dozens of superbugs. Besides TB, infections caused by other bacteria, parasites, and viruses can also become drug resistant.

Introduction

Ask Americans what public health threats they fear, and they might name AIDS, flu, mad-cow disease, or even bioterrorism. Chances are, they will not mention tuberculosis (TB). Most people think of TB as something from history textbooks, like smallpox or polio. After all, we have antibiotics now, and we can prevent or cure TB, right?

Not necessarily. Even with antibiotics, TB remains a formidable foe, circulating among one-third of the world's population.[1] It is highly infectious, difficult to detect, and often hard to kill. It may lurk in the body for decades before suddenly activating. Although uncomplicated TB can be defeated with antibiotics, it takes six to nine months of treatment with powerful drugs that often have unpleasant side effects.

If a person stops taking medication too soon or skips doses, a much scarier disease can result: drug-resistant TB. If the patient gets sick again, he or she may face a much more difficult road to recovery, and may also pass drug-resistant strains of the disease on to other people. This is one reason new varieties of TB are now loose in the world and resistant to multiple antibiotics.

Other infectious organisms are also becoming drug resistant. They are aptly named "superbugs." Malaria, caused by a parasite, has been around since ancient times, but it still kills over one million people worldwide every year.[2] Methicillin-resistant *Staphylococcus aureus* (MRSA) is a new version of an old bacterial infection that was once easily cured by antibiotics. It gets its name from the fact that the drug methicillin is now powerless against it. Drug-resistant varieties of pneumonia and other infections have arisen as well.

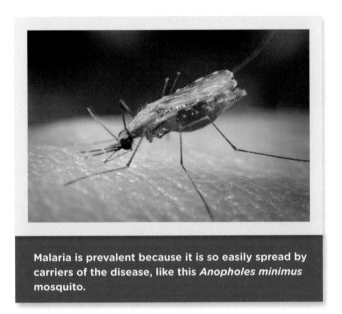

Malaria is prevalent because it is so easily spread by carriers of the disease, like this *Anopholes minimus* mosquito.

This book covers TB and other superbugs—what they are, how they affect the body, how they are diagnosed and treated, and how drug resistance has affected their course. Stories of children and adults with TB and other infectious diseases show how real people deal with these stubborn and sometimes devastating illnesses.

CHAPTER ONE

Understanding Tuberculosis

I n January 2007, Andrew Speaker, a thirty-one-year-old lawyer from Atlanta, fell and landed on his rib cage. He went to the doctor for an X-ray, which revealed an abnormality, but not from the fall. After several other tests, Andrew was finally diagnosed in March with tuberculosis (TB). He began taking antibiotics. Two months later, his doctors informed him that he actually had multidrug-resistant TB (MDR-TB), a much more serious type that is resistant to most drugs. According to Andrew, he felt fine and had no symptoms. He said the doctors told him he was not contagious, and although they said they would prefer if he did not travel, they never ordered him not to.

So Andrew traveled. He was scheduled to get married, and on May 12, he flew to Paris and then to Greece for his wedding. He was honeymooning in Europe when the Centers for Disease Control and Prevention (CDC), a United States government agency, called him to say that his original diagnosis had been wrong. What he actually had was extensively drug-resistant TB (XDR-TB), a rare, much more serious, sometimes incurable disease. They told him to either check into a European hospital or hire a private plane to take him back to the United States so he would not expose other passengers. Unable to afford a private plane and worried that he would not get good care in Europe, Andrew flew on a commercial flight to Montreal, Canada. Then he rented a car, drove across the border into the United States, and checked himself

Andrew Speaker was diagnosed with drug-resistant TB, which cannot be treated with traditional antibiotics.

into a New York City hospital. Even though they had been alerted, the Canadian border patrol failed to detain Andrew because he did not look sick.

When CDC officials found out that Andrew had boarded a commercial flight, they held a press conference and warned the public that an American passenger with XDR-TB was traveling from Europe to Canada. They even announced Andrew's name. The news caused an international uproar.

After staying in the New York hospital for a few days, Andrew was transported in a medevac plane to CDC headquarters in Atlanta. He was then taken to National Jewish Hospital in Denver, Colorado, which specializes in treating TB and other lung conditions. Andrew was the first American to be quarantined by the federal government since 1963. At the hospital, he was isolated from other patients and given potent antibiotics. Then on July 4, the hospital announced that Andrew did not have XDR-TB after all. The diagnosis of MDR-TB, a still serious but more treatable form, was correct. The fact is, MDR-TB and XDR-TB are not any more contagious than regular TB; they are just harder to treat. But no matter what type of TB Andrew had, everyone around him had been exposed.

In July, Andrew had surgery to remove a diseased part of his lung. He remained in the hospital for eight weeks, taking powerful antibiotics, which he would have to continue taking for the next two years. Because he was young and otherwise healthy, the doctors expected him to make a full recovery. But even though Andrew was getting better, his life was falling apart. He got hate mail and death threats. His legal practice fell apart. His marriage came to an end when it had barely begun. Several people who had been sitting near him on the plane sued him (although in the end, none actually caught TB from him). In 2009, Andrew himself sued the CDC for invading his privacy, destroying his reputation, and causing his marriage to end.

This incident was called the TB Scare of 2007, and it brought attention to the growing problem of drug-resistant infections.[1]

What Are Bacteria?

Bacteria are single-celled organisms that resemble spirals, balls, or rods when viewed under a microscope. They are so tiny that millions could fit on a pencil eraser! Ninety-nine percent of bacteria are harmless, and many are actually good for people, supplying vitamins, helping the body digest food, and destroying cells that cause disease.

But one percent of all bacteria make people sick. Tuberculosis, some types of pneumonia, and many infections acquired in hospitals are caused by bacteria. These bacteria multiply in the body and destroy tissue. They are also infectious, meaning they can be passed on to other people.

Most bacteria cells multiply rapidly, as often as every twenty minutes. But TB bacteria cells are slowpokes, taking sixteen to twenty hours to reproduce. This can be frustrating for researchers growing TB for lab experiments and for doctors and patients waiting for a diagnosis.

Tuberculosis is caused by *Mycobacterium tuberculosis*, a rod-shaped aerobic bacterium. (*Aerobic* means the bacteria need oxygen to live and grow.) The bacterium is also called tubercle bacillus or Koch's bacillus, after Robert Koch, the scientist who first isolated it.

Bacterial Shapes

Bacilli   Cocci   Spirilla

Bacteria come in many different shapes and sizes. *Mycobacterium tuberculosis* is rod-shaped and known as a bacillus.

WHAT IS TB?

Tuberculosis is an infectious disease caused by a type of bacterium called *Mycobacterium tuberculosis*, or *M. tuberculosis* for short. The TB bacteria mainly attack and damage the lungs, but they can also get into the bloodstream and invade other parts of the body, such as the kidneys, spine, and brain. If not treated properly, TB can be fatal. In the early 1900s, before antibiotic drugs were developed, TB was one of the leading causes of death in the United States.

Although TB affects people of all ages, races, and socioeconomic backgrounds, it is not well understood. Many people think TB occurs only in underdeveloped countries, or only in poor people, or that the disease has been eradicated. The fact is, TB is one of the most deadly diseases in the world and has been for centuries. In spite of modern drugs, scientists have never come close to eradicating it.

According to the CDC, one-third of the world's population has TB, and nearly 2 million people die from the disease every year. Although TB rates have been decreasing in the United States, there were still 12,904 cases reported in 2008.[2]

Tuberculosis remains a frightening and perplexing disease. Why? Because in recent years, several types of TB bacteria have emerged that are immune to the antibiotics commonly used to kill them. This development is called drug resistance (see "When Bugs Resist Drugs"). Tuberculosis can also lurk in the body for years without being contagious or causing symptoms, then suddenly activate. When this happens, people get sick and can unknowingly spread TB to others.

These and other factors have caused TB to remain a major health concern around the world. But the more people know about the disease, the better they can protect themselves and others and help slow TB's spread.

When Bugs Resist Drugs

When people are small children, they often make a face and try to resist taking medicine when they are sick. But another kind of drug resistance is much more serious. It occurs when the "bugs" that cause a disease resist the drugs used to treat it.

Drug resistance occurs naturally over time, as bacteria, viruses, and other disease-causing microbes (microscopic organisms) change. They develop resistant genes, pass these traits on to their offspring, and begin to protect themselves against antimicrobial drugs, like antibiotics. The drugs kill off most of the microbes, like they are supposed to, but the tougher ones stay alive and get stronger. Soon, these tough guys—known as superbugs—start reproducing and their descendents become the major microbes that cause infections. Then diseases like TB that were once treatable become harder, or even impossible, to cure.

Humans help speed this process along. When patients ignore their doctor's orders and only take half their medicine because they feel better, they stay sick, but the superbugs get stronger and healthier. The same thing happens when doctors do not prescribe antimicrobial medicine for a long enough time or prescribe it when it is unnecessary or inappropriate. These and other misuses of drugs encourage the microbes that cause infection to flourish and pass from person to person. No wonder they call them superbugs!

Take all of the medication your doctor has prescribed, even if you are feeling better.

TYPES OF TB

Pulmonary TB, the most common and infectious type, occurs in the lungs. About 85 percent of people with TB have this type.[3] Pulmonary TB causes a cough that lasts three weeks or longer and produces blood, chest pain with breathing or coughing, fever, weight loss, lack of appetite, fatigue, and night sweats.

TB bacteria can also infect other organs. This is called extra-pulmonary TB. Symptoms vary depending on the organ involved. For example, skeletal TB, also called Pott's disease, usually involves the spine, causing back pain and stiffness. Paralysis of the legs occurs in up to half of untreated cases. In TB meningitis, bacteria quickly invade the base of the brain and the meninges (covering of the brain). They cause headache, seizures, coma, and death if left untreated. Miliary or disseminated TB is a severe type of TB that spreads to many organs in the body, dotting the organs with hundreds of minute tubercles. Early researchers thought these tubercles looked like millet seeds, a type of grain. Symptoms depend on the organs involved, but can include cough, fatigue, fever, shortness of breath, sweating, and weight loss. Miliary TB was a death sentence before antibiotics, but now most people recover.

Ten to fifteen million people in the United States are thought to have latent TB infections.

Tuberculosis can also be classified as either a latent infection or an active TB disease. A latent infection lives in the lungs without making a person sick or contagious. This occurs in nine out of ten people.[4] A latent infection may stay in the lungs forever without becoming active, may become active after several years, or may activate only a few weeks after infection. Ten to fifteen million people in the United States are thought to have latent TB infections.[5] Active TB disease makes people sick and can spread to others.

Only Humans Get TB

Not so. Many mammals, especially cattle, deer, bison, and goats, can get a form of TB called *Mycobacterium bovis*, or bovine TB. However, it is extremely rare for a human to catch TB from an animal, even if the person eats meat or drinks milk from an infected animal.

M. bovis is generally found in lung tissue, not meat (muscle tissue). However, all meat should be thoroughly cooked to kill bacteria. Pasteurizing milk at high temperatures destroys TB and other bacteria. Inspection systems for cattle, meat, and milk also help protect consumers. Today, bovine TB has been virtually eradicated, with less than 0.002 percent of U.S. cattle being infected.[6]

Animals get TB the same way humans do—by inhaling infected respiratory droplets from each other. But they can also get it by eating feed that has been contaminated with TB by other infected animals. If an animal is found to have TB, it must be removed from the herd and destroyed.

Besides *M. bovis*, animal TB can also be caused by *M. tuberculosis*, and another type of TB, *M. avium*. *M. tuberculosis* mainly infects humans, but hogs, cattle, and dogs can also get it. *M. avium* affects hogs, cattle, and all species of birds.

Cows, goats, bison, and other animals can get TB, too.

HOW IS TB TRANSMITTED?

Only people who have active TB in their lungs are infectious. They can spread TB when they cough, sneeze, talk, or sing, spewing tiny, bacteria-containing droplets into the air. These droplets stay airborne for several hours, so anyone nearby can inhale them into their lungs.

Sneezing without covering one's mouth casts thousands of droplets into the air, spreading germs.

Coughing produces 3,000 droplets; so does talking for five minutes or singing for one minute. But a single sneeze generates tens of thousands of respiratory droplets into the air, reaching people up to ten feet away.[7] Infection with TB begins when these droplets reach the alveoli (air sacs) of the lungs.

Surprisingly, TB is not especially easy to catch through casual contact. People cannot get it by shaking hands with an infected person or by touching eating utensils, clothing, or other objects someone with TB has handled. Even drinking from the same glass or kissing an infected person will not transmit TB, because the bacteria are not present in saliva. It is only in the sputum (phlegm) coughed up from the lungs.

HOW TB INVADES THE BODY

What happens when TB bacteria are inhaled into the body? They head straight for the lungs. Knowing how the bacteria get there and how the body tries to stop them will help you understand the infection process.

During breathing, air is inhaled through the mouth or nose. Air then travels down the pharynx (throat), larynx (voice box), trachea (main breathing tube), and bronchi, two large tubes that lead into each lung. The lungs are large, soft, spongy organs on either side of the heart. The right lung is bigger than the left and contains three lobes. Because the heart tips toward the left side, there is not as much room in the chest for the left lung, so it only has two lobes.

Once inside the lungs, the bronchi branch like a tree into even smaller airways called bronchioles, which are only one-half of a millimeter in diameter. At the end of these threadlike tubes are tiny balloonlike air sacs called alveoli. Each lung contains millions of alveoli, which look like tiny bunches of grapes when viewed under a microscope. Oxygen and carbon dioxide gas exchange takes place in the alveoli. Carbon dioxide from the rest of the body is transported through blood vessels to the

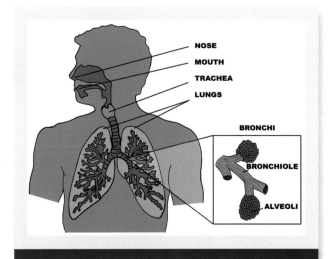

The lungs are the largest organ in the respiratory system and are responsible for transferring oxygen to the circulatory system.

alveoli, and then oxygen in the alveoli is transported by blood to all cells in the body. The alveoli are where the inhaled TB bacteria lodge—if they make it that far.

First Line of Defense

The body puts up a good fight when threatened with bacterial invasion. The first line of defense is the nostrils, which contain hairs designed to trap invaders like TB bacteria. Bacteria that make it through the forest of hairs then have to navigate a river of gooey mucus covering the lining of the nostrils. The bacteria are propelled by hairlike structures called cilia, which beat up to 1,000 times a minute and move the bacteria to the back of the throat and eventually into the mouth. There, the bacteria can be coughed up, sneezed out, or swallowed. If bacteria are swallowed, stomach acids will usually kill them.

Immune System to the Rescue

If bacteria manage to invade the alveoli in the lungs, the body's immune system sends in the big guns. White blood cells called macrophages storm in, surround the bacteria, and try to kill it. Most types of bacteria are easy to kill, but TB bacteria have a thick, waxy coating that is hard to destroy. They stay alive and

What Are Tubercles?

A tubercle (pronounced TOO-ber-kul) is a small, firm nodule or lump characteristically found in the lungs of TB patients. The word comes from the Greek word *tubercule*, meaning "little swelling" or "nodule." Also called granulomas, tubercles occur when the immune system summons white blood cells called T cells and macrophages, which clump together around TB bacteria in the lungs and try to kill them.

multiply inside the macrophages. Compared to most other types of bacteria, which multiply every twenty to forty minutes, TB bacteria multiply very slowly, only every sixteen to twenty hours. Because bacteria are easier to kill when they are multiplying, the macrophages do not get many opportunities to strike. In addition, TB bacteria have evolved very effective mechanisms for resisting the macrophage attacks by the immune system.

In an effort to kill the bacteria, macrophages begin clustering together inside the alveoli. Other white cells, called T cells, join the fight and add to the cluster. A few weeks after infection, the clustered cells form small, hard swellings called tubercles, which is why TB bacteria are also called tubercle bacilli (see "What Are Tubercles?").

As more and more cells cluster, the tubercles may grow larger and destroy lung tissue around them. When lung cells die, soft areas resembling cheese form inside the tubercles, while tough scar tissue forms around them. When TB bacteria stay imprisoned inside these walls, alive but no longer multiplying quickly, a person does not have symptoms and is not contagious. This is latent TB.

Whether a person develops the active form of the disease after it infects the lungs depends largely on the strength of the immune system. People with weak immune systems—such as young children, the elderly, or those with HIV (the AIDS virus)—can rarely fight off the infection and will develop active TB. People with strong immune systems usually keep TB in a latent condition and may never know they are infected. Or, they may find out inadvertently when they have a positive reaction to the TB skin test (see Chapter 5, "Testing and Treatment"). Other people with TB can move from the latent phase to the active phase throughout the course of the disease.

What happens when the immune system is too weak to wall off the bacteria? The bacteria escape from the tubercles and multiply like crazy, destroying lung tissue and replacing it with soft, cheeselike material, which eventually liquefies. Dead cells and bacteria mix with mucus and get carried up the airways, leaving behind cavities and scar tissue in the lungs. The lungs start to disintegrate, causing telltale signs and symptoms.

Although TB may kill a person quickly, it is more apt to cause long, gradually worsening illness.

The first sign of TB is a cough, caused by excess mucus in the bronchi. At first, coughing only occurs in the morning, to rid the lungs of mucus that accumulated during the night. People may think they just have a bad cold. Eventually, the cough gets worse and people notice blood in the sputum they expel. This is caused by TB bacteria breaking out of the alveoli and entering the capillaries. Breathing becomes labored as more and more lung tissue is destroyed and fewer undamaged alveoli exist to take in oxygen and send it to the body cells.

The cells cannot function without sufficient oxygen, so the whole body suffers damage. The person feels weak and tired and loses weight. Although TB may kill a person quickly, it is more apt to cause long, gradually worsening illness. By the time a doctor diagnoses TB, a person may have unknowingly infected as many as fifteen other people.

WHO GETS TB?

Most people who get coughed or sneezed on by someone with active TB do not become infected themselves. Generally, a person must remain in close contact for a long period of time with someone harboring an active TB infection. This is why TB occurs most often in households, workplaces, schools, nursing homes, dormitories, and prisons. Any cramped, poorly ventilated area where many people are together for hours and days is a breeding ground for TB. Under the right conditions, one person with an active case may infect ten to fifteen others within a year.[8]

Officials at the CDC keep track of TB cases in the United States. In 2008, they found that TB rates were the lowest since reporting began in 1953. But they also discovered that Americans born in foreign countries had TB almost ten times more often than native-born Americans. Asian Americans had the highest TB rates, with 25.6 cases per 100,000 people. One reason for this is that many immigrants come from countries with high rates of TB and have latent infections when they arrive.[9]

The TB rates for blacks, Hispanics, and other racial and ethnic groups were found to be higher than for whites. Rates of TB are also different for men and women. In all races, TB rates decline as women get older, but they rise as men get older. The CDC has concluded that these differences probably have more to do with people's economic, social, and medical conditions than their race or gender.[10]

WHO IS MOST AT RISK?

Anyone can get TB, but people with weakened immune systems or those who live or work in crowded, poorly ventilated spaces are especially vulnerable. Here are the groups at risk:

- Babies and young children
- People over sixty-five, especially those with other illnesses or living in nursing homes
- People with HIV, cancer, diabetes, or other diseases
- People taking certain drugs, such as those for arthritis or cancer chemotherapy, which suppress immune function
- People with poor nutrition, such as those with eating disorders that cause low body weight
- People who abuse drugs or alcohol, which leads to poor nutrition
- People who live or have lived in places with high TB rates, such as Africa, India, China, or Indonesia
- People who live or work in migrant or refugee camps or homeless shelters
- People who live or work in nursing homes, prisons, or immigration centers
- People without good access to medical care because of low income, long working hours, homelessness, or recent immigration
- People who travel internationally.[11]

TB AROUND THE WORLD

The World Health Organization (WHO) declared TB a global health emergency in 1993. Why is TB still so prevalent? Scientists believe the HIV pandemic is largely to blame. People infected with HIV have severely weakened immune systems, leaving them defenseless against TB and many other infections. The latest statistics, from 2007, estimate that 33 million people in the world have the HIV virus.[12] Of these, about one-third are also infected with TB.[13]

According to the American Lung Association's 2007 data, one-third of the increase in global TB cases over the last five years can be attributed to the HIV pandemic. About one in ten people infected with the TB bacteria will develop active TB sometime in their lives, but the percentage increases if the person has the HIV virus.[14]

According to the WHO, an estimated 9.2 million new cases of active TB occurred in 2006 and approximately 1.7 million deaths resulted from TB worldwide.[15] Although nearly every nation experiences TB, it is a more severe problem among developing nations. Famine, war, displacement of people, the emergence of drug-resistant strains (types), and other factors contribute to both TB and HIV. Developing nations account for 95 percent of all TB cases and 98 percent of all TB deaths worldwide. Overall, 15 percent of people with active TB die from it. But the death rate varies from 7 percent in industrialized countries to 20 percent in Central and South America and 35 to 40 percent in parts of Asia and Africa. More than 50 percent of TB victims die in parts of Africa where health care is lacking and HIV is prevalent.[16]

WHEN TB GOES UNTREATED

Untreated TB can have grave consequences. It kills more than half of its victims, usually from respiratory failure caused by lung damage. Other vital organs that were attacked when the disease spread can also shut down, causing death.[17]

Although latent TB is not contagious, many people with this type of TB are time bombs waiting to go off. Unless they happen to have a TB test (for example, if a health insurance company requires it), they may never know they are infected because they do not have symptoms. However, if their immune systems are weakened by another illness, they may develop an active case and spread the disease to others.

Some people with active TB start treatment, but when they begin to feel better, they do not finish the recommended course of antibiotics. Doing this can have severe consequences. For one thing, the person will not be cured of TB and will continue infecting others. Partial treatments can also cause the bacteria to become resistant to the drugs, so any future treatment is much more demanding and rigorous. You will read more about the growing problem of microbial resistance throughout this book.

Untreated TB can have grave consequences. It kills more than half of its victims, usually from respiratory failure caused by lung damage.

The good news is that TB is usually treatable, but patients must follow their doctor's orders precisely. People diagnosed with latent TB need to take one drug for nine months to prevent active disease from occurring. People with active TB need to take several different drugs for six to twelve months because they have a large amount of bacteria in their bodies.

DRUG-RESISTANT TB

Now for the bad news: TB is becoming increasingly drug resistant. Two new types of TB have emerged: MDR-TB and XDR-TB. Very expensive antibiotics taken for up to two years can kill MDR-TB, but patients can remain contagious for a long time, exposing more people. This type was discovered in 1985 in South Africa. The second type, XDR-TB, was discovered in South Africa in 2006 and is resistant to almost all available TB drugs, making it extremely hard to treat.

What Are Antibiotics?

Antibiotics are drugs that kill or weaken bacteria that cause infectious diseases. At first, they were made from molds, but now they are produced synthetically, with chemicals. Different antibiotics are designed to target different types of bacteria. They either zero in and kill bacteria, or they keep them from multiplying by preventing them from building cell walls. Either way, they do not harm the body's cells. First-line antibiotics are the ones usually used to treat an infection. Second-line antibiotics are the big guns, brought in when first-line drugs stop working, such as in drug resistance.

This magnified image shows rifamycin crystals. These crystals are synthetically produced to make antibiotics that are used to treat tuberculosis and other diseases.

Different antibiotics cause different side effects. Some common ones are nausea, diarrhea, and vaginal yeast infections in women. Some uncommon, severe side effects are hearing loss, kidney and liver damage, and colitis (inflammation of the large intestine). Blood tests are used to monitor kidney and liver function.

Antibiotics are big business. In 1954, 2 million pounds of antibiotics were produced in this country. Today, more than 50 million pounds are produced every year.[18]

No one is sure how many people are infected with drug-resistant TB worldwide, but some studies indicate that, in certain regions of the world, at least 20 percent of all TB cases are MDR-TB and of these, 10 percent are XDR-TB, or 2 percent of the total.[19] In the United States, eighty-three cases of XDR-TB were reported between 1993 and 2007.[20] Most people with drug-resistant TB were born in foreign countries.

Unfortunately, finding new antibiotics to fight TB has not been a priority of pharmaceutical companies since the 1950s. Most companies put their research efforts into finding profitable drugs that people will take every day for the rest of their lives, such as those to fight diabetes, high cholesterol, or HIV/AIDS. The apparent lack of interest in developing new TB drugs angers and worries people working to eradicate TB. Many believe that rich countries ignore TB because it mainly occurs in poor countries, and that most research money is being poured into AIDS at the expense of TB. The fact is, TB kills almost as many people as AIDS; TB outbreaks do occur in industrialized countries, including the United States; cheaper and more convenient travel expose increasing numbers of people to TB; and drug-resistant strains are developing that cannot be killed with forty-year-old drugs. What's more, people infected with HIV are highly susceptible to TB, so finding new TB drugs would also help keep AIDS patients well. No matter how one looks at TB, the problem is too serious to ignore.[21]

If drug resistance continues unchecked, does this mean the rates of infection and death from TB and other infectious diseases will eventually get as high as they were before antibiotics were invented? "It's a threat," said Dr. Anthony Fauci, director of the National Institute of Allergy and Infectious Diseases, during a 2007 interview. "If we get asleep at the switch, then it's going to happen. But we should not allow that to happen," he said.

Dr. Fauci added that he is confident the drug companies and research community will begin working together and step up their efforts to develop new drugs to combat TB and other infectious diseases.[22]

FAMOUS PEOPLE WHO HAVE HAD TB[23]

Name	Occupation
Emily Brontë (1818–1848)	British writer, best known for her novel *Wuthering Heights*
Frederic Chopin (1810–1849)	Polish composer/pianist
Henry David Thoreau (1817–1862)	American author of *Walden*
Stephen Crane (1871–1900)	American novelist
Paul Laurence Dunbar (1872-1906)	African-American poet
George Orwell (1903–1950)	British author, well-known for novels *Animal Farm* and *1984*
Vivien Leigh (1913–1967)	British actress; well-known roles included Scarlett O'Hara in *Gone with the Wind*
Nelson Mandela (1918–)	Former president of South Africa and anti-apartheid activist

CHAPTER TWO

Understanding Other Superbugs

When antibiotics were first developed in the 1940s, everyone from scientists to the general public thought these "wonder drugs" would wipe out TB and other bacterial infections. But only a few years later, doctors noticed that some of their patients were not responding to antibiotics as well as they had at first. Doctors were dismayed to discover that some of the bacteria were mutating so that antibiotics were not as effective at destroying them. By the 1990s, several new strains of bacteria had evolved that the usual antibiotics could not kill. These bacteria were labeled *drug resistant*. They have also been called superbugs.

Besides TB, several other bacterial diseases have developed drug-resistant strains. Drug-resistant viral and parasitic diseases have surfaced as well.

FRIGHTENING BACTERIAL INFECTIONS

Ninety-nine percent of bacteria are harmless, but one percent can make people sick and even kill them. These bacteria are categorized as gram-positive and gram-negative based on their cellular structure. Both types of harmful bacteria can become resistant to antibiotics.

In 1882, Danish bacteriologist J.M.C. Gram discovered a way to tell different types of bacteria apart. He stained the bacteria with a dye called crystal violet, which appears purple-brown under a microscope. He called bacteria that were stained by the crystal violet gram-positive. Bacteria that were not stained were termed gram-negative and appeared red.

This test is still used today and is usually the first one done to see what type of bacteria is causing an infection. Identifying the type of bacteria can help doctors decide which type of antibiotic will work best.

M. tuberculosis is classified as gram-positive but often stains only slightly.

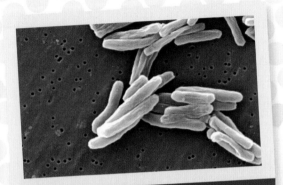

The *M. tuberculosis* bacterium, as seen under a scanning electron microscope, is gram-positive, though it often only stains slightly.

GRAM-POSITIVE BACTERIA

MRSA

Methicillin-resistant *Staphylococcus aureus*, or MRSA (pronounced "MER-suh"), is a potentially deadly bacterial infection that invades different parts of the body. The type of bacterium that causes it, commonly called staph, is gram-positive and lives on the skin, on desks, and on a thousand everyday objects. About one-third of all people have it on their skin or in their noses without being sick. This is called being colonized. These people can pass the germ to others.[1]

According to a 2007 report from the CDC, about 94,000 people in the United States develop serious MRSA infections every year, and about 19,000 die.

Staph is usually harmless, but when the bacteria get into the body, usually through a cut, they multiply and cause an infection. The incubation period (time between infection and when symptoms occur) is one to ten days. Fortunately, most staph infections are easy to treat with antibiotics.

One exception is MRSA. This strain of staph is resistant to the antibiotic methicillin as well as other antibiotics in the penicillin family, including amoxicillin, oxacillin, and cephalexin. When MRSA was first discovered in England in 1961, methicillin was the drug used to test and treat *S. aureus* infections. However, in the early 1990s, oxacillin became the agent of choice for treating staph, as the bacteria slowly began to develop resistance to methicillin

MRSA can be caught as easily as by sharing towels with someone who is infected.

after the drug's discovery. The acronym MRSA is still used because of the historic role methicillin played in the evolution of this bacteria, even though methicillin is not even prescribed today in the United States.

MRSA now occurs worldwide. According to a 2007 report from the CDC, about 94,000 people in the United States develop serious MRSA infections every year, and about 19,000 die.[2]

MRSA occurs most often in hospitals, nursing homes, and other health-care settings, affecting the elderly and others with weakened immune systems. Patients often become infected through open wounds, urinary catheters, or IV lines. At least 60 percent of staph infections occurring in U.S. hospitals are due to MRSA, and these numbers are rising here and around the world.[3]

Unfortunately, MRSA is occurring more and more in healthy people outside of hospitals. This is called community-associated MRSA. According to the CDC, in 2007, 14 percent of people with MRSA had acquired it in a community setting.[4]

MRSA is transmitted three ways:

- by touching an infected area on another person's skin
- by sharing razors, towels, or other personal items with an infected person
- by touching surfaces contaminated with MRSA bacteria, such as a phone or computer keyboard

What Is VRSA?

Vancomycin-resistant *Staphylococcus aureus*, or VRSA (pronounced VER-suh), is a gram-positive bacterium that is resistant to—you guessed it—vancomycin. It was first identified in Japan in 1996, and has since been found in hospitals in England, France, Asia, Brazil, and the United States. The first case in the United States was in 2002. This infection is still very rare—only seven cases had been reported in the United States by 2007.[5]

Like MRSA, VRSA is transmitted through the skin. It has similar symptoms and can also be deadly if untreated. The difference is that VRSA cannot be cured with vancomycin, the drug used to treat MRSA. It requires antibiotics that are often less effective and more toxic than most antibiotics against non-resistant bacteria. Some that have been used are rifampin, gentamicin, and chloramphenicol. VRSA patients may also qualify for emergency use of experimental drugs that are being tested by the U.S. Food and Drug Administration.

People who develop VRSA typically have chronic diseases that weaken their immune systems. Many have also taken vancomycin for a long time. So far, the disease has occurred only in hospitals, but experts are worried it might eventually spread into the community, like MRSA.

People need only touch an area infected with MRSA, then touch a small cut, pimple, or other open area on their skin to catch the infection. This is why MRSA is more likely to occur among people in close contact, such as those who share bathrooms or locker rooms.

All staph skin infections, including MRSA, start out innocently, looking like insect bites, pimples, or boils. Without treatment, the skin bumps can quickly become deep, painful, and pus-filled. The infection can then travel deep into the body, infecting the bones, bloodstream, heart, lungs, and other organs and tissues. This is when MRSA becomes deadly.

Symptoms of a deeper infection—called invasive disease—depend on the site of infection. For example, MRSA that infects the brain causes sleepiness, headaches, or a stiff neck. MRSA that infects the lungs can cause cough, chest pain, and breathing difficulties. If caught early, MRSA can be treated successfully with the antibiotics vancomycin and teicoplanin.

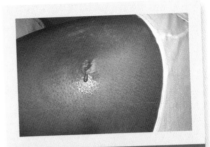

This abscess was caused by the MRSA bacterium.

Streptococcal Pneumonia

The gram-positive *Streptococcus pneumoniae* bacterium was first recognized in the 1800s as a cause of bacterial pneumonia. The bacteria can lead not only to pneumonia but also to relatively minor illnesses such as sinusitis (sinus infection) and otitis media (ear infection), as well as life-threatening diseases like bacteremia (bloodstream infection) and meningitis (brain infection). It is the most common bacterial cause of these diseases.

fact OR fiction

A MRSA Infection Looks Like a Spider Bite

True! At least that is what many people first think that it is. Staph infections of the skin can look pretty nasty, and people often think they were bitten by a brown recluse spider. When doctors hear this, it raises a red flag for MRSA. When staph enters the skin through a cut, it can cause redness, swelling, and blisters, boils, or bumps filled with draining pus. People should see their doctors immediately if they have these symptoms.

Although the total number of *S. pneumoniae* cases in the United States is dropping, the prevalence of drug-resistant strains has been rising since 1987. A decade ago, *S. pneumoniae* caused 60,000 cases of invasive disease in the United States every year, and as many as 40 percent of these were caused by bacteria that did not respond to one or more antibiotics. The number of infections decreased after 2001, when the pneumococcal conjugate vaccine was introduced, but the problem of drug resistance remains.[6] See Chapter 4 for more information about this vaccine, which is given to infants and young children.

Few statistics are available on the extent of pneumococcal infection worldwide or in the United States. However, the WHO estimates that 1.6 million people died of the disease in 2005. People at highest risk for pneumococcal infection are children under age two, adults over age fifty-five, and people of any age with weakened immune systems.[7]

Like TB, *S. pneumoniae* is spread from person to person through airborne respiratory droplets from the nose or mouth of an infected person. The infected person may be sick or may be a carrier with no symptoms. The incubation period is usually one to three days. Symptoms vary depending on the location of the infection, and may include fever and earache (otitis media), headache and stiff neck (meningitis), and fever and shortness of breath (pneumonia).

Without treatment, this infection can cause death or permanent problems such as hearing loss (with otitis media), learning disabilities, and nerve damage (with meningitis).

GRAM-NEGATIVE BACTERIA

Since 2000, several gram-negative bacteria have become drug resistant. So far, these bacteria have caused sickness almost exclusively in hospital settings, but experts fear they will spread into the community like MRSA.

Meat Is Loaded With Antibiotics

Sad, but true. Meat-producing animals are now raised in "animal factories," in densely packed pens where antibiotics are added to their feed to make the animals grow faster and to keep them from getting sick due to crowded, unsanitary conditions and unnatural diet. Cows are naturally grass eaters, and factory-raised cows that are fed corn tend to get sick more often. Incredibly, the amount of antibiotics given to animals in the United States is eight times greater than the amount given to people![8]

Does this lead to the development of drug resistance? Evidence shows that healthy animals exposed to low dosages of antibiotics over long periods are inviting bacteria to develop resistance. After the animals are killed, these resistant bugs show up in the meat people buy at the grocery store. In 2001, the *New England Journal of Medicine* reported that 20 percent of the ground meat in the Washington, D.C., area was contaminated with *Salmonella*, and 53 percent of these bacteria were resistant to at least three antibiotics.[9] *Salmonella* can cause food poisoning when meat is consumed rare or medium rare.

Eating contaminated meat is one way drug-resistant bacteria can pass from animals to humans. A second way is when livestock workers handle feed, animals, or manure, then transfer bacteria to other people. A third route is via manure-contaminated groundwater and soil.

One solution is cutting out or reducing antibiotics in cattle feed. Eighty health organizations support this, and some restaurants, including McDonald's, are working with suppliers to decrease antibiotic use by their meat producers.

Infections from gram-negative bacteria are very drug resistant, almost impossible to treat, and have long, nearly unpronounceable names. Some examples are *Acinetobacter baumanii, Klebsiella pneumoniae,* and *Pseudomonas aeruginosa.*

No one is sure how many people in the United States and around the world get sick or die from these gram-negative, primarily hospital-borne infections because they are not regularly reported to the CDC. However, CDC data from 2002 show that of the estimated 90,000 deaths annually in U.S. hospitals from bacterial infections, more than 70 percent were caused by bugs resistant to at least one common antibiotic.[10]

Gram-negative bacteria live on the skin and inside the bodies of healthy people and also in soil and water. They can be spread from person to person, often when health-care workers do not wash their hands between caring for patients. Hands contaminated with the bacteria can then contaminate medical equipment, like urinary catheters or feeding tubes, and enter a patient's body. The bacteria can also live on moist or dry surfaces for several days.

Klebsiella is normally found in the colon or large bowel, but when it gets outside the bowel, it can cause infection if health-care workers get feces on their hands and do not wash properly. *Acinetobacter* is found in soil and water and thrives in warm, humid climates. In 2004, approximately 30 percent of all wounded soldiers returning from Iraq and Afghanistan were infected with this bacterium.[11] As a result, evacuation facilities and military hospitals have also become contaminated.

Besides these wounded soldiers, other people at risk include those with weakened immune systems: the very young and very old, those in intensive care units, and patients with burns or organ transplants. One antibiotic, colistin, has been marginally successful in treating these infections, but it does not always work and can damage the kidneys.

HOW REAL PEOPLE DEAL: A MODEL'S TRAGIC DEATH

Brazilian model Mariana Bridi da Costa had everything to live for. At age twenty, she was on her way to becoming a top model and had just become Brazil's entry in the Miss World pageant. But then she got a common illness that turned deadly.

In late December 2008, Mariana was not feeling well, so she went to the doctor. She was diagnosed with kidney stones, given medicine, and sent home. But she got worse instead of better. Mariana returned to the doctor in early January, and this time she was diagnosed with a urinary tract infection and hospitalized. Tragically, by the time doctors realized what kind of bacterium was causing her infection, it had entered her bloodstream.

Mariana was infected with *Pseudomonas aeruginosa*, which caused a deadly chain reaction. A condition called sepsis occurred, resulting in a life-threatening drop in her blood pressure. Also, the bacteria in her blood caused a system-wide infection and triggered her immune system to overreact, causing insufficient blood flow to her organs and extremities.

After Mariana entered the hospital, her condition swiftly got worse. The doctors gave her strong antibiotics, but the drugs did not kill the bacteria. Her organs began to fail because they were not getting enough blood, and the doctors were forced to remove her kidneys and part of her stomach. They also amputated her hands and feet because the blood had stopped flowing there and the skin and muscle tissue had died. Mariana was placed on kidney dialysis and a ventilator,

Mariana Bridi da Costa was infected with *Pseudomonas aeruginosa*, which is resistant to many antibiotics. She died within a month of getting sick.

which breathed for her because her lungs were failing.

She could only communicate with her eyes, but she managed to signal to her family that she wanted to live.

But on January 21, Mariana died. During her illness, news of her condition had spread around the world. The outpouring of curiosity and concern was evident—her Web site received 15,000 hits in two days, causing it to crash.

How could a bacterial infection kill a healthy young woman in only a month? For one thing, *P. aeruginosa* is notoriously hard to treat because it is naturally resistant to many antibiotics. It also easily mutates, causing more drug resistance. On top of this, doctors still have many questions about sepsis and what triggers it.

"We know a lot about what happens once a patient contracts the illness, but we know very little about what causes it," said Dr. Greg Martin of Emory University in Atlanta. He said that sepsis is the tenth leading cause of death in the United States.[12]

Generally speaking, symptoms of infection include a high fever, chills, and flulike symptoms. Patients with wounds have drainage that contains pus. Infection with *Klebsiella* typically causes the patient to cough up thick, blood-tinged phlegm, called currant jelly sputum. If the bacteria get into the bloodstream, they can quickly travel to every organ in the body, causing many different symptoms and often killing the patient. Symptoms usually occur forty-eight hours or more after hospital admission and up to thirty days after admission for patients who were infected in a surgical wound.

A PERSISTENT PARASITIC INFECTION

A parasite is an organism that lives off other organisms. Diseases caused by parasites range from those that can kill you, like malaria, to those that are simply annoying, like head lice (see "What Is Pediculosis?", p. 40). Parasitic infections are some of the most common infections in the world, but there are no vaccines against them. Controlling them depends on drugs or chemicals. Unfortunately, many parasites are developing antibiotic resistance. Malaria, a leading cause of death in developing countries, is one of them.

Malaria (pronounced muh-LARE-ee-uh) is a potentially fatal disease usually caused by a bite from the female *Anopheles* mosquito. The infection is caused by four parasites— *Plasmodium falciparum* (the most deadly), *P. vivax, P. ovale*, and *P. malariae*—which destroy a person's red blood cells. The mosquito bites a person infected with one of these parasites, drinks a small amount of infected blood, and then passes the infection on to the next person it bites.

A young boy sits with his sister while she waits to be treated for malaria in Kenya. Malaria is a leading cause of death in Africa.

Because malaria is transmitted by blood, people can also catch it through blood transfusions and organ transplants, or by sharing needles or syringes with someone who is infected. Malaria can also be transmitted to an infant before or during delivery.

Worldwide, 300 to 500 million cases of malaria occur each year, killing more than one million people. In children under five, it is the fourth leading cause of death in developing countries. In Africa, a child dies of malaria every thirty seconds.[13] Malaria is prevalent in parts of Africa, Asia, the Middle East, Central and South America, the Pacific Islands, Haiti, and the Dominican Republic.

Although malaria was thought to be eradicated in the United States in the early 1950s, about 1,300 people are still diagnosed with the disease every year.[14] Almost all of them recently immigrated from or traveled to countries where malaria is common. Between 1957 and 2003, the CDC recorded sixty-three cases of malaria from local mosquitoes. This occurs when people who contracted malaria in other countries are bitten by mosquitoes in this country. These mosquitoes then become infected and bite other people.[15]

What Is Pediculosis?

Pediculosis is an infestation of parasites commonly called head lice, which are tiny, wingless insects that live on the human scalp and feed on blood. They are spread by head-to-head contact and possibly by sharing combs, pillows, or hats. Anyone can get them, but they are most often found in children ages four to eleven. Twelve million people in the United States get head lice every year.[16]

The main symptom of head lice is itching. The lice or their eggs may also be visible, especially behind the ears or at the nape of the neck. Until recently, lice have been easy to get rid of with over-the-counter or prescription medicines such as permethrine. However, the bugs are starting to become resistant to these drugs. Researchers at the University of Massachusetts Amherst have found that ivermectin, a drug used to treat intestinal worms and plant parasites, is 100 percent effective in killing head lice resistant to other drugs. However, ivermectin has not been approved by the FDA for use against head lice, and there is no indication when or if FDA approval may happen.

Head lice, which have been relatively easy to treat in the past, are becoming increasingly resistant to the drugs used to kill them.

Signs and symptoms of malaria usually occur ten days to four weeks after infection. However, some parasites can lie dormant in the liver for up to four years before a person gets sick. Malaria causes severe flulike symptoms, including fever, shaking, chills, headache, fatigue, muscle aches, nausea, vomiting, diarrhea, and jaundice (yellowing of the skin and eyes). Untreated malaria can be deadly.

People can take drugs to prevent malaria, but there is still no vaccine against it. The usual treatment for malaria is the drug chloroquine, but some strains of *P. falciparum* and *P. vivax* have become resistant to it. When patients do not get better on chloroquine, several other drugs, including antibiotics, are tried. Unfortunately, in some areas of the world, *P. falciparum* has become resistant to almost all drugs currently used.

Because malaria is transmitted by blood, people can also catch it through blood transfusions and organ transplants, or by sharing needles or syringes with someone who is infected.

PERVASIVE VIRAL INFECTIONS

Viruses are tiny bits of protein that hold genetic material. They are much smaller than bacteria. Viruses invade the body's cells and begin reproducing wildly, eventually killing them. A few viruses lie dormant for weeks, months, or even years before they do their dirty work. Some viruses are not serious, like the ones that cause the common cold. Others are deadly, like HIV, the AIDS virus. All viruses are infectious.

Viruses are hard to treat. Because they live inside our normal cells, they are difficult to destroy without damaging our own cells. Drugs that kill viruses are called antiviral medicines, but there are not many of these. Some drugs and vaccines have been developed to prevent and treat the flu and a few other viral infections, but these diseases continue to cause some of the most serious infections known to man. Like bacteria and parasites, viruses are developing drug resistance.

HIV/AIDS

The human immunodeficiency virus (HIV) causes acquired immunodeficiency syndrome (AIDS) and severely weakens the body's immune system so it cannot fight off infections. Because of this, people with HIV are extremely vulnerable to other infections, especially TB.

HIV is causing TB rates to increase around the world. Why? Because people with HIV are not well enough to keep TB latent, so they develop contagious, active TB. By the same token, TB is further weakening people's immune systems, causing HIV to develop into full-blown AIDS. The two infections are fatally intertwined.[17]

According to the WHO, 40 million people in the world are infected with HIV or AIDS, and about one-third of them are co-infected with TB. In a given year, people with HIV are up to fifty times more likely to develop TB than people who are HIV-negative.[18]

The CDC estimates that up to 1.1 million people in the United States are living with HIV or AIDS.[19] It occurs most often in men who have sex with men and in African Americans, but a large proportion of heterosexuals, and white men and women are also infected with HIV, and these numbers are increasing.

The AIDS virus is present in blood and other body fluids. It is most often spread sexually, through intercourse or oral sex, or nonsexually by sharing needles or syringes during drug use. It is not spread by casual contact, like shaking hands or kissing.

Some people with HIV have no symptoms, but others may have a sore throat, fever, or swollen glands shortly after they are infected. These symptoms go away on their own in a couple of weeks, but the virus continues to replicate and destroy the immune system until the person becomes sick again. People may not realize they are infected for as long as ten years following infection and spread the virus during this period.

HIV and AIDS cannot be spread through kissing.

The advanced stage of HIV disease is AIDS. Experts believe that everyone with HIV eventually develops AIDS, but some people stay well for a long time. Eventually, HIV cripples the immune system and opens the door to numerous health problems, including extreme fatigue, rapid weight loss, diarrhea, and purple skin growths, rashes, and opportunistic infections, which include certain types of infections that normally don't occur in people without HIV. Eventually, it is one of these infections that kills a person with HIV.[20]

There is no cure for HIV or AIDS, but people who know they are infected can take a combination of drugs that can prevent or suppress viral replication and enable their immune systems to recover. However, failure to take these medications properly invariably gives rise to drug resistance. About 20 to 40 percent of people are found to have drug-resistant strains of HIV when they are first diagnosed, before they have taken the drugs for very long. This leads researchers to believe that a person with a drug-resistant strain of the virus can pass this strain on to another person.[21]

Influenza

Influenza, known as the flu, is a highly contagious respiratory infection caused by one of several different viruses. It is transmitted through airborne respiratory droplets and

What Is an Epidemic? What Is a Pandemic?

An epidemic occurs when a group or region suddenly has more cases of a disease than usual during a given period of time. It is usually the result of a severe outbreak. A pandemic is like an epidemic, but on a larger scale, and it also must involve an infectious disease. When an infectious disease becomes widespread and affects a whole region, a continent, or the entire world, it is called a pandemic.

The H1N1 flu was defined as a pandemic by the World Health Organization because it spread rapidly from Mexico, to the United States, and then around the world. HIV/AIDS, TB, and malaria are also considered pandemics. Cancer, diabetes, obesity, and other diseases affect billons of people around the world, but they are not infectious, so they are considered epidemics.

by touching surfaces contaminated with the virus and then touching the eyes, nose, or mouth. Symptoms appear eighteen to seventy-two hours after infection, and the illness lasts an average of five days.

Every year, the flu infects 5 to 20 percent of the U.S. population. More than 200,000 people end up in the hospital, and 36,000 die every year.[22] Most deaths are in those with weakened immune systems, such as young children and the elderly.

Three types of seasonal flu usually occur: Type A, Type B, and Type C. Types A and B are responsible for the usual flu epidemics that cause muscle aches, coughing, stuffy nose, headache, and fever. Type C flu is less severe and the rarest of the three types. All flu viruses mutate over time, so researchers develop new vaccines based on the strain of flu they expect to occur the following winter. Each flu vaccine contains all three flu viruses.

All strains of the seasonal flu are treated with the drug Tamiflu, although Type A began showing resistance to this drug during the 2008–2009 flu season. However, other flu treatments are available, and the number of resistant cases was very small.

Unfortunately, a new flu virus emerged in April 2009. Called novel H1N1, it started in Mexico, moved on to Texas and California, and then spread to every state and throughout the world. By July 2009, more than 80,000 people had been infected worldwide and 337 people had died. In the United States, 33,902 people were infected and 170 had died.[23]

At first, novel H1N1 was called the swine flu because it resembled a virus that normally occurs in pigs. But researchers soon realized that the virus is actually a combination of flu viruses normally found in pigs, birds, and humans. It is a brand new strain of flu.

Every year, the flu infects 5 to 20 percent of the U.S. population. More than 200,000 people end up in the hospital, and 36,000 die every year.

The novel H1N1 virus is different from seasonal flu in a couple of important ways. A high proportion of people between ages five and twenty-four get it, rather than the very young and very old. It also causes diarrhea and vomiting, symptoms not usually seen with seasonal flu. Other symptoms of novel H1N1 are the same as for seasonal flu. Despite what some

Unlike the seasonal flu, which affects the very young and very old, the H1N1 flu generally affects those between the ages of five and twenty-four.

rumors suggest, it spreads the same way any other flu virus spreads, and one cannot catch it by eating pork, drinking water, or swimming in a pool.

Tamiflu has also been successful in treating the novel H1N1 flu, although a handful of drug-resistant cases were reported in July 2009. Experts are not surprised, because a lot of doctors are prescribing Tamiflu to treat mild cases of flu or to family members at risk of catching the disease when one or more other family members are infected. Widespread use of Tamiflu can cause the virus to mutate, resulting in more serious infections of novel H1N1 in the future. A vaccine to prevent H1N1 was developed in the summer of 2009, and public distribution began in late October 2009.

CHAPTER THREE

The History of TB and Other Superbugs

n the nineteenth-century science fiction novel *War of the Worlds* by H.G. Wells, Martians invade England. Traveling in tripod fighting vehicles, they destroy everything in their path. Even an atomic bomb does not stop them. Then suddenly, the Martians begin to die. It turns out they had no resistance to earthly germs—bacteria killed them.

In real life, however, bacteria are often the enemies, not the heroes, and antibiotics and other drugs come to the rescue. But seventy years after the discovery of antibiotics that saved millions of humans from bacterial diseases, researchers are once again looking for wonder drugs. Drugs that once conquered TB and other infections are becoming powerless against a new breed of drug-resistant microbes. The story is still unfolding.

In the *War of the Worlds* by H.G. Wells, Martians in tripod fighting vehicles wreaked havoc on planet Earth. They were eventually defeated by bacteria.

THE ORIGINS OF TB

Humans have been living with *M. tuberculosis* since prehistoric times. In 2007, Turkish scientists found a 500,000-year-old skull of the species *Homo erectus* with what appear to be TB scars. These scars have also been found in the skeletons of prehistoric man from the early Neolithic period (4000 B.C.) and in the spines of Egyptian mummies dating from 3000 to 2400 B.C. Genetic studies reveal that TB has been present in the Western hemisphere for at least 2,000 years. Most of today's TB strains probably originated in East Africa 30,000 years ago and then spread

Scars in the skull of this *Homo erectus* were caused by an early form of TB.

around the world when people migrated. The earliest physical evidence was found in Peru's Paracas-Caverna culture of about 750 B.C. to 100 A.D.

From the dawn of recorded history, humans have been describing the ravages of TB. The world's first organized library, Mesopotamia's Library of Assurbanipal, contained medical records from the seventh century B.C. that describe a patient who coughs incessantly and spits up blood. Babylonian clay tablets more than 2,000 years old also described TB symptoms. Some evidence of a special hospital for TB patients existed as early as 1000 B.C.

Greek and Roman history in the fourth century B.C. makes reference to a disease called *phthisis* (pronounced TEE-sis), meaning "to waste away or decay." To this day, specialists in the field of TB are called phthisiologists. Hippocrates, the famous Greek physician, noted that the widespread disease phthisis was almost always fatal.

Ibn Sina (980–1037 A.D.), a Persian physician, was the first to recognize TB as a contagious disease. He thought it spread through soil and water and developed a quarantine system to limit transmission. In his great work, the *Canon of Medicine*, Ibn Sina summarized all existing medical knowledge, adding his own notes and interpretations, including information on TB.

SCOURGE OF THE INDUSTRIAL REVOLUTION

From the 1600s to the 1800s, as Europe, and later America, became industrialized, TB epidemics killed large numbers of people. Dutch doctor Franciscus Sylvius described structures in the lungs of TB patients that he called "tubercles" in a book published in 1679. In the 1700s, TB caused one out of four deaths in Europe and was one of the most deadly diseases in America, too.[1]

TB Is Hereditary

No! The disease is spread from person to person when respiratory droplets are spewed into the air through coughing, sneezing, or talking. If several family members living together get TB, it is simply because they are in close contact, not because they inherited the disease.

In 1720, *A New Theory of Consumptions* was published by English physician Benjamin Marten. He wrote that TB was caused by "wonderfully minute creatures" and could be transmitted if people were around an infected person for a long time. He believed that the disease rarely spread during short periods of contact.

The first recorded TB epidemic occurred in the eighteenth and nineteenth centuries. During the Industrial Revolution, the rural poor flocked to Europe's cities, but working conditions in the factories were terrible and living conditions just as bad. People lived in dark, damp, close quarters and endured long work hours and poor nutrition. The Industrial Revolution created the ideal conditions for TB, and it began to spread like wildfire.

In spite of the bleak reality of living with TB and the poor prospects of surviving it, people of this era romanticized the disease. Artists, musicians, and writers were thought to be touched with creative genius in the late stages of TB, which was called consumption. Other names for TB were the white plague and wasting disease, because victims became very pale and lost so much weight they seemed to waste away.

TB Was Romanticized in the Past

The degree to which TB was romanticized in the nineteenth century is hard to comprehend in today's world. Operas and literary works were filled with pale, weak heroines who languished in bed, reciting poetry. Examples from literature include Fantine in *Les Misérables*, Mimi in *La Bohème*, and Camille from *La Traviata*. Tuberculosis was so glamorized that healthy teenage girls actually tried to look limp and pale.

John Keats, born in 1795, was perhaps the most revered poet of the Romantic period. Known for his energy, humor, and zest for living, Keats started out studying medicine and gave it up to write poetry. Two of his most famous poems are "Ode to a Nightingale" and "Ode on a Grecian Urn."

John Keats died of tuberculosis at the age of twenty-five.

Keats's parents died when he was only fourteen, his mother of TB. His brother John died of the disease in 1818. Shortly afterward, Keats began having sore throats and was diagnosed with TB, too. But he was healthy enough to write most of his major works that year, an outpouring of at least a dozen poems that are now considered some of the greatest in English literature.

In 1820, Keats traveled to Europe to stay with his doctor, James Clark. Clark was convinced Keats's health problems were digestive, not caused by TB, so he suggested regular exercise instead of rest. Late that year, Keats began coughing up blood and then had a serious hemorrhage. Dr. Clark realized that Keats had TB and began treating the disease.

In those days, the cure for TB was as bad as the disease. Keats was prescribed a near-starvation diet and frequent bleedings (cutting the skin and letting blood flow). He finally became bedridden and died in 1821 at the age of twenty-five. After his death, his sad story captured people's imaginations. The artist Joseph Severn even drew a sketch of how he imagined Keats looked while dying. The poet became the symbol of the TB patient who is creative, introspective, and romantically dead at an early age.[2]

PIONEERS IN TB RESEARCH

The rise of TB to epidemic status drew many doctors and researchers to study it. Tuberculosis was recognized as a distinct disease in the 1820s, and the German physician Johann Lucas Schönlein gave it its permanent name in 1839.

The French doctor René-Théophile-Hyacinthe Laënnec invented the stethoscope in 1816, an indispensable tool for describing the symptoms of heart and lung disease. His book, *De l'Auscultation Mediate*, published in 1819, featured a huge section on diseases of the lungs. Laënnec's work with the stethoscope led to two theories about TB. The first was that TB was a hereditary disease. It was triggered by poor living conditions, malnutrition, moral depravity, and a "TB taint" inherited from parents.

The second theory was that tubercles (hard nodules) in TB patients' lungs contained poisonous matter. French scientist Jean-Antoine Villeman tested this theory by implanting material from tubercles under the skin of a rabbit. New tumors developed. But when he published his findings in 1865, no one was impressed.[3]

In 1863, a French researcher, Casimir-Joseph Davaine, was the first to observe microscopic organisms in the blood of diseased people. But he could not prove that these organisms caused diseases. That feat would fall to the German microbiologist Robert Koch, who set out to demonstrate that specific microbes caused specific diseases. His discovery was later termed the "germ theory."

In 1882, Koch became convinced that a type of bacterium caused TB. He developed new staining methods to help visualize bacteria and also new ways of growing it, using a flat dish invented by his colleague, Julius Richard Petri. The Petri dish is still used in labs today. In 1882, Koch discovered the tubercle bacillus—the rod-shaped bacterium *M. tuberculosis* that causes TB. Then he concentrated on finding a vaccine to prevent the disease.[4]

What Was the Sanatorium Movement?

In the pre-antibiotic era, TB sufferers who could afford it were prescribed a change of scenery. They were sent to special hospitals just for TB patients, called sanatoriums. In the mid-nineteenth century, these hospitals began springing up in the United States, Canada, and Europe, often in the mountains where the air was pure.

Doctors prescribed lots of sunlight and fresh air, even in the winter. Sea air, mountain air, cold air, and warm air were all suggested as cures. So was a rich, nourishing diet with plenty of milk, cream, and eggs, and lots of rest. Most patients stayed at these facilities at least a year.

Gustav Hermann Brehmer opened the first sanatorium in 1859 in the mountains of Germany. In America, the great sanatorium advocate was Edward Trudeau, a doctor who was diagnosed with TB in 1873. After visiting Saranac Lake, New York, he was inspired to build Adirondack Cottage Sanatorium, where patients lived in private cottages and followed a strict diet and exercise regimen. By the early twentieth century, there were more than 400 sanatoriums in the United States.[5]

The Adirondack Cottage Sanatorium offered TB patients the chance to rest in a healthy environment. In 1954, it closed after antibiotics were discovered to effectively treat the disease.

Although Trudeau offered free medical care and charged very low rent, most sanatoriums were expensive. Less elegant institutions were opened for charity patients, and people also hired nurses to teach them how to cure their TB at home. Some patients were advised to construct platforms for their beds so they could sleep in the open air on the roofs of tenement buildings, even in cold weather, since cold fresh air was often prescribed for TB patients.

After streptomycin was put into general use as an antibiotic treatment for TB in 1947, the TB sanatoriums began closing.

ATTEMPTS AT TREATMENT AND PREVENTION

Before the development of antibiotics, there was no effective treatment for TB. Folk remedies included eating wolf's liver boiled in wine, weasel blood, pigeon dung, and live snails. Physicians tried exercise, bed rest, starvation diets, rich foods, tonics, tranquilizers, opium, cod-liver oil, gold salts, and Fowler's solution, a tonic full of arsenic. Other strange treatments included inhaling oxygen and hydrogen sulfide gas (which smells like rotten eggs) while sitting in a glass cabinet. The drugstores sold Piso's Cure for Consumption and Schenck's Pulmonic Syrup.[6]

A popular treatment starting in the mid-nineteenth century was the sanatorium, a hospital/health spa exclusively for TB patients. Sanatoriums were still operating into the mid-twentieth century.

Prevention of disease and infection is a more modern concept than treatment of disease. For centuries, doctors did not realize that washing their hands before and after touching patients would help keep infectious diseases from spreading. They even performed surgery without gloves while wearing street clothes. Not until the nineteenth century and the discovery that germs spread infection and disease did washing and disinfection to prevent infection become more common. Similarly, efforts to prevent tuberculosis rather than just treat it did not begin to pick up steam until the founding of the National Anti-Tuberculosis Society in 1904. Public health measures that promoted good hygiene, less crowded living conditions, and detection and community care helped reduce the number of TB cases beginning around this time, but the death rate from TB did not decline until the use of antibiotics after 1947.

THE SEARCH FOR A VACCINE

The word "vaccination" comes from the Latin term *vaccina*, meaning "cowpox." In 1798, an English doctor named Edward Jenner noted that milkmaids who contracted cowpox, a fairly mild disease, appeared immune to the much more serious disease smallpox, which killed or disfigured millions of people. So Jenner inoculated an eight-year-old boy with cowpox and then injected him with the much more virulent smallpox virus. The boy did not contract smallpox. This unethical experiment led to worldwide vaccinations that eliminated smallpox from the planet by 1979. Scientists and researchers began to research vaccines that might protect people from many other diseases.

The search for an effective TB vaccine obsessed many early researchers. After Robert Koch identified *M. tuberculosis* in 1883, he began searching for a vaccine. Around this time, Louis Pasteur created a successful rabies vaccine by injecting weakened live bacteria into people. This technique, called attenuation, did not cause infection but still provoked an immune response in the body, protecting the vaccinated person from infection. The Sabin vaccine against polio, first given in 1962, was also an attenuated vaccine.

In the late nineteenth century, Koch developed a vaccine for TB using the same process. He called it tuberculin. In 1890, he published a paper hinting that he had created a vaccine that might be helpful in diagnosing and curing TB, which also protected animals from TB and could heal tubercles in the lungs. As news of the vaccine spread, doctors and TB patients began to beat a path to Koch's laboratory in Berlin. Americans and Europeans were thrilled at the discovery of the substance they referred to as lymph. They hoped this vaccine would end TB.

But the vaccine did not work as expected, and people continued to die from the disease after being vaccinated. Europeans soon became disillusioned with the vaccine, although it was used in the United States until the 1920s. Eventually, tuberculin was successfully used as a test for the presence of *M. tuberculosis*.

Koch received numerous awards in his lifetime and was responsible for many important discoveries in the field of microbiology, including advances in the diagnosis, prevention, and treatment of anthrax, cholera, malaria, and other infectious diseases besides TB. In 1905, he received the Nobel Prize in Physiology and Medicine for his discovery of *M. tuberculosis.*

Robert Koch developed a vaccine for TB. He also coined the phrase "germ theory."

Although tuberculin failed as a vaccine, it served as a springboard for the next generation of vaccine seekers. In 1920, French physicians Albert Calmette and Camille Guérin announced their creation of a TB vaccine. They took a virulent form of the bovine tuberculosis bacillus, *M. bovis*, which affects cattle but can infect humans, and transferred it from culture to culture to weaken the bacteria. After transferring cultures every three weeks for several years—for a total of 231 transfers—they finally had their vaccine, which they tested in rabbits, guinea pigs, cattle, and horses. They called the new vaccine Bacillus Calmette-Guérin, or BCG.[7]

An oral form of BCG vaccine was tested in France, Holland, Belgium, and the Soviet Union. In 1928, the Health Committee of the League of Nations accepted the vaccine as an effective form of treatment against TB. In spite of a setback in Germany, where live TB germs were mistakenly given to a group of infants (many of whom died), the international community recommended the vaccine. An injectable form is still in use today, though its efficacy remains unclear.

United States health officials were reluctant to use the BCG vaccine because of questions about its safety and effectiveness. It seemed to work only against very specific kinds of TB infections: the miliary form of TB and TB that produces meningitis in children. They also felt it might give people a false sense of security and cause them to abandon basic hygiene. To this day, the BCG vaccine is rarely used in this country. The U.S. approach is to test people at high risk for TB regularly and then treat them with antibiotics if they are infected, rather than use mass immunizations.

ENTER ANTIBIOTICS

In 1928, Alexander Fleming, a Scottish microbiologist, noticed mold growing in a laboratory dish of *Staphylococcus* bacteria. The bacteria around the mold were dead. Without realizing it, Fleming was looking at penicillin.

Fifteen years later, Fleming and two other scientists purified, tested, and produced penicillin in time to treat wounded soldiers during World War II. Drug companies began mass producing penicillin, and by war's end, enough of the drug was made to save millions of lives and cure several deadly bacterial infections, including the sexually transmitted disease syphilis. Other antibiotics followed, and optimism that infectious diseases would be eradicated bloomed.

Tuberculosis, however, proved a tough nut to crack. Penicillin did not kill it. Researchers got a break in the early 1940s, when Rutgers University professor Selman Waksman and colleagues, including Albert Schatz, isolated organisms in soil that were capable of slowing the growth of several penicillin-resistant bacteria, including the tubercle bacillus. The experiments that followed yielded the first antibiotic effective against TB: streptomycin. The drug was tested on patients in the winter of 1944–45, and eliminated *M. tuberculosis* from their sputum. Streptomycin was put into general use in 1947. Selman Waksman took sole credit for the discovery, for which he won a Nobel Prize, but later court cases proved that Albert Schatz was a co-discoverer; the two men are jointly credited today.[8] Besides killing TB bacteria, streptomycin is also effective against typhoid fever, bubonic plague, cholera, and other deadly infections caused by gram-negative bacteria.

THE ROOTS OF DRUG-RESISTANT TB

Unfortunately, streptomycin caused severe side effects in some patients, such as kidney failure and deafness. More ominously, scientists noted a new phenomenon: some strains of TB were becoming resistant to streptomycin. People who were thought to be cured of TB had relapses after a few months of treatment. Luckily, new TB drugs were being developed. One drug, para-aminosalycic acid (PAS), was approved for use in the late 1940s. For several years, combining PAS and streptomycin cured TB and prevented the emergence of drug-resistant strains.[9]

In 1952, a third drug, isoniazid, was introduced. It is still a mainstay in TB treatment. Combining this drug with PAS and streptomycin cut treatment time from two years to eighteen months. Over the next few decades, other drugs were developed and added to the treatment regimen with varying degrees of success. In 1960, rifampin was put on the market. This breakthrough drug successfully killed very slowly dividing TB bacteria. Combined with at least two other TB drugs, it cut treatment time down to a mere six months.[10]

These drugs, the BCG vaccine, and anti-TB campaigns launched by the United Nations and the WHO, were stamping out TB in both industrialized and developing countries. By the 1960s, the incidence of TB was beginning to drop even in Africa, where widespread poverty and development issues had long made the battle against TB difficult.[11]

Health officials believed they had eradicated TB. But little by little, the disease began reappearing all over the world. Why? Because strains of *M. tuberculosis* were emerging that were resistant to all the major TB drugs. By the late 1970s, rates of TB were rising again, especially in developing regions, such as Africa and Southeast Asia. But the number of TB cases was also rising in industrialized countries, such as England and the Soviet Union.

THE NEW YORK CITY EPIDEMIC

No country is immune to TB, including the United States. After 1953, when isoniazid was put on the market, the number of TB cases started to drop steadily. So government funding for TB prevention, screening, and treatment programs was

This 1992 cover of *Newsweek* magazine signaled the return of tuberculosis as a health threat in the United States.

drastically cut, and drug companies stopped developing new TB drugs. Cases of TB reached an all-time low by 1985, and the disease was thought to be all but eradicated.

In 1985, public health officials got a nasty surprise: TB cases were on the rise again. The increase was especially evident in New York City, where a number of social factors converged to create the perfect environment for a new TB epidemic. These factors were unusually high rates of unemployment, homelessness, over-crowding, and poverty. Prisons were filled with drug users, and tenements were filled with poor families. Immigrants were arriving in record numbers, carrying latent TB, which later blossomed into active TB because of harsh living conditions. Also on the rise were HIV infections, which cripple the immune system and leave people powerless against TB.[12]

From 1983 to 1993, the incidence of TB more than doubled in New York City, with 3,811 cases in 1992, many of them in hospitalized patients with HIV.[13] To make matters worse, many patients had multidrug-resistant TB (MDR-TB), meaning at least one, and sometimes two or three, of the usual TB drugs did not work for them. Patients most likely to have MDR-TB are those who have been treated for TB previously, those with HIV, and those who inject drugs. During the early 1990s, one in ten cases of TB in New York City was MDR-TB.[14]

To combat the epidemic, New York City assembled a TB task force. People were diagnosed and treated free of charge, were isolated if they had TB, and were given appropriate drugs if they had MDR-TB. Between 1996 and 2000, 80 percent of infected people got the care they needed, stopping the epidemic in its tracks. This was helped by the development in 1998 of the first new TB drug in twenty-five years, called rifapentine.

By 2002, TB rates in the city had reached an all-time low of 1,084, but stopping the epidemic had cost about one billion dollars.[15]

DRUG-RESISTANT TB IN OTHER COUNTRIES

Unfortunately, impoverished countries that did not have billions of dollars to mobilize task forces continued to see a rise in TB cases and deaths. Although the WHO has established a committee to reduce the cost of the newest, most effective drugs, called second-line drugs, to treat MDR-TB, the price of treatment can still be up to 1,400 times the cost of regular treatment with older drugs, known as first-line drugs.[16]

Even more alarming, a 2006 study in Africa found a second, even more virulent strain of drug-resistant TB, termed XDR-TB. This strain is sometimes untreatable. It has now been found in more than fifty countries on six continents, and affects at least 50,000 people per year. Of these, about 30,000 die.[17]

HISTORY OF OTHER DRUG-RESISTANT DISEASES

The history of other drug-resistant diseases ranges from stories of ancient infections, like malaria, to brand-new diseases like the H1N1 flu, which surfaced in 2009.

MRSA

The antibiotic methicillin was introduced in 1959 to treat staph infections resistant to penicillin. But in 1961, the first cases of methicillin-resistant *S. aureus* (MRSA) were discovered in hospitals in England. During the 1970s and 1980s, resistant strains appeared in hospitalized patients all over the world, including the United States.

No one knows exactly how MRSA emerged in community settings. But now this potentially deadly infection is making healthy people in different communities sick, not just those with weakened immune systems in hospitals. Community-acquired MRSA is called CA-MRSA, and hospital-acquired MRSA is called HA-MRSA.[18]

Streptococcal Pneumonia

S. pneumoniae was first isolated in 1881 by two researchers working independently: French chemist Louis Pasteur and U.S. Army doctor George Sternberg. It was first called pneumococcus and then *Diplococcus pneumoniae*. In 1974 it was given its current name. In 2001, the pneumococcal vaccine was introduced and given to children in the United States and other industrialized countries, which caused the number of serious infections to decrease. Another vaccine is now available for adults over age sixty-five and other high-risk people. Although the number of cases has subsequently dropped, penicillin-resistant and multidrug-resistant strains have begun to emerge, making the bacteria harder to kill.

Klebsiella pneumoniae, seen here in an agar culture, is one infection that has succesfully resisted many drugs, making it almost impossible to treat.

Gram-Negative Bacterial Diseases

Hospital-acquired infections, also called nosocomial infections, and the bugs that cause them are nothing new. According to the CDC, 2 million patients get these infections every year and nearly 88,000 die.[19] What *is* new is the increasing number of drug-resistant strains of these types of infections that have started occurring in hospitals across the country. The biggest culprits are gram-negative bacteria, which are basically untreatable. Sometimes the immune system can fight them off, but often such infections are fatal.

The first such gram-negative bacterium was *Klebsiella pneumoniae*, found in a New York City hospital patient in August 2000. Only one drug, colistin, was known to cure it, but it was rarely used because it could damage the kidneys. By October 2003, thirty-four patients had gotten *Klebsiella* infections, and nearly half had died, even though meticulous infection control procedures were followed. Similar infections soon occurred in other New York City hospitals, as well as in hospitals in other states. These infections are still occurring today.[20]

The plot thickened when the drug-resistant bacteria *Acinetobacter baumanii*, found in soil and water, started infecting about 30 percent of soldiers returning from Afghanistan and Iraq. The bacterium, which thrives in hot, humid climates, is now common among patients in U.S. military hospitals.

Studies around the world show how fast these bacteria spread. According to Dr. Christian Giske, a clinical microbiologist from Sweden, 50 to 60 percent of hospital-acquired bacterial infections in southern Europe are drug resistant. "There are now a growing number of reports of cases of infections caused by gram-negative organisms for which no adequate therapeutic options exist," he said. "This return to the preantibiotic era has become a reality in many parts of the world."[21]

Malaria

Malaria comes from the Italian word for "bad air," although it is actually transmitted through a mosquito bite. The disease was first described in 2700 B.C. in ancient Chinese medical writings. Back then, malaria killed thousands, depopulating whole cities and rural areas. In the sixth century B.C., a medical text from India credited insect bites for transmitting malaria, while writers during Roman times (around 450 A.D.) blamed the disease on swamps—which is where mosquitoes often breed.

In 1946, chloroquine was put on the market and is still the drug of choice against malaria today. By 1951, malaria was eradicated in the United States.

This seventeenth-century engraving depicts the country of Peru (boy) giving a cinchona branch to Science (warrior on the left). The bark of the cinchona tree is used to make quinine, a centuries-old cure for malaria.

Through the ages, various remedies were used, without success. But two early cures actually worked. In 340 A.D., Chinese scientists documented the anti-fever powers of quinghao, an ingredient in the powerful antimalarial drug artemisinin, developed in 1971. In the early seventeenth century, missionaries learned of a medicinal tree bark made by South American Indians that also cured "fever." This bark, ground up and put into a liquid, was used successfully to treat malaria for many years, but it was not given its modern name quinine until 1820. Quinine is still one of the most effective malarial treatments.

In 1880, the organism that causes malaria was discovered by Charles Louis Alphonse Laveran, a French army surgeon. While stationed in Algeria, he noticed parasites in the blood of a malaria patient. Around the same time, Camillo Golgi, an Italian neurophysiologist, discovered two forms of malaria: one that caused fever every day, and one that caused fever every third day. He also discovered that parasites were released into the bloodstream when fever occurred.

Between 1890 and 1897, scientists in Europe and the United States discovered four malaria parasites that infect humans: *Plasmodium vivax*, *P. malariae*, *P. ovale*, and *P. falciparum*. In 1897, Ronald Ross, a British officer in the Indian Medical Service, found that these parasites could be transmitted from infected patients to mosquitoes. Then in 1899, Italian investigators demonstrated that mosquitoes infected with malaria could pass the disease on to humans. The mystery of transmission was solved.

Once the cause of malaria was known, people could take measures to curtail it. Besides giving quinine as a medicine for it, they kept mosquitoes from breeding by draining pools and swamps and cutting high grass that hid standing water. In 1910, the Panama Canal was completed, due in part to fewer workers contracting malaria and being unfit to work. Once mosquitoes were controlled in the area, the number of workers with malaria decreased to from 21,000 to 5,600.[22]

In 1914, the United States government started a similar campaign to control malaria, especially in the southern states, where the disease was most common. New drugs and chemicals were also effective. In 1939, the insecticide dichloro-diphenyl-trichloroethane (DDT) was first used to kill mosquitoes and thus control malaria during World War II. Afterwards, it was used in high-risk areas of the United States. In 1946, chloroquine was put on the market and is still the drug of choice against malaria today. By 1951, malaria was eradicated in the United States. But it remained a problem in other areas of the world.

In 1955, the WHO proposed a global campaign against malaria that included house spraying with insecticides and treating people with antimalarial drugs. The program helped in some countries, but the malaria problem returned when the program stopped. Some regions, such as sub-Saharan Africa, were left out of the program entirely. Over the years, malaria reemerged as parasites became resistant to drugs and insecticides. Wars, lack of funding for programs, lack of cooperation from communities, and lack of a malaria vaccine has made eradication impossible. Simply trying to *control* malaria is now the main goal.

HIV/AIDS

The history of AIDS in the United States is brief but alarming. The disease was first recognized in this country in 1981. Gay men in New York and California were developing infections and cancers that seemed resistant to any treatment. Similar cases were reported later among drug users, Haitians, and hemophiliacs (people with a disorder that causes excessive bleeding). In 1982, the mysterious disease was given a name: acquired immune deficiency syndrome or AIDS.

Advances in understanding AIDS moved as swiftly as the disease spread. In 1983, doctors at the Pasteur Institute in France identified the retrovirus that caused AIDS. In 1985, a blood test was developed to diagnose the virus, and in 1986, it was named human immunodeficiency virus, or HIV. In that same year, nearly 3,000 people died in the United States from the disease. By 1995, the number of deaths had risen to over 48,000 in a single year.[23] The country had an epidemic on its hands.

No one really knows the exact origins of AIDS, but there are numerous theories. Researchers discovered in 1999 that HIV-1 (the most common cause of AIDS in the United States) was similar to a virus called SIV found in chimpanzees in Africa. How was the disease transferred to humans? The most common theory is that humans killed and ate the diseased chimps, and the virus mutated into HIV-1. Over time, it may then have transferred from person to person by means of contaminated needles.[24]

However it began, it seems likely that Africa was where AIDS originated and first spread. In 2007, scientists presented data showing that HIV-1 was brought to Haiti from the Congo by a single person around 1966. Probably another single individual brought the virus to the United States between 1969 and 1972. Eventually, the virus took hold, developed drug-resistant strains, and the rest is history.

Influenza

Historical records have described flulike pandemics for at least the last four centuries. Since 1900, three flu pandemics and several "pandemic threats" have occurred. The worst outbreak in history was the Spanish flu in 1918, which infected 20 to 40 percent of the world's population, killing at least 50 million people.[25] Other flu outbreaks occurred after vaccines were developed and were not as severe. They include the 1957 Asian flu, which killed about 2 million people around the world; the 1968 Hong Kong flu that killed approximately one million people;[26] and the 1977 Russian flu that also killed about one million people.

In 1997 the avian flu infected a few hundred people in Hong Kong and killed six. It was passed from chickens to humans, so all chickens in Hong Kong were slaughtered. No new human cases occurred after that. This virus has not become pandemic, but the fact that birds continue to carry it, that it infects humans, and that the virus can mutate is an ongoing concern.

Vendors were forced to slaughter millions of chickens to prevent the avian flu from spreading during a 2001 outbreak in chickens in Hong Kong.

Drug resistance and influenza did not become a worry until the last few years, with the increased use of Tamiflu, a drug used to prevent and treat seasonal flu. It is also being used to treat the newest flu virus, novel H1N1, which started in Mexico in April 2009, spread to the United States, and then spread worldwide. Three months later, more than 80,000 people had been infected and 337 had died.[27] This flu is a combination of viruses normally found in pigs, birds, and humans. Although only a few drug-resistant cases had been reported by July 2009, widespread use of Tamiflu may cause the virus to mutate, resulting in more serious infections of novel H1N1 in the future. Researchers developed an H1N1 flu vaccine, which became available to the public in October 2009.

CHAPTER FOUR

Preventing TB and Other Superbugs

A Chinese proverb says: "The superior doctor prevents sickness, the mediocre doctor attends to impending sickness, and the inferior doctor treats actual sickness."

While it is helpful to treat someone who is sick, it is even more beneficial to prevent that person from getting sick in the first place. During the last few centuries, some of the world's most brilliant doctors and researchers have dedicated their lives to studying infectious diseases, working on disease prevention. These people, along with other medical professionals and public health officials, are still working feverishly today. But when one problem gets solved, another problem, often worse, crops up.

No one knows this better than the people who "attend to impending sickness." In the world of infectious diseases, these words aptly describe the looming threat of drug-resistant diseases—epidemics that are waiting to happen or already have.

The major burden of preventing these diseases falls on the shoulders of medical professionals. But people can do more than wring their hands and wait for the worst. We need to be more aware of how infectious diseases are spread and how to decrease the chances of transmitting them or getting them. A big part of prevention has to do with having good health habits, like frequent hand washing, and using common sense. Preventing drug resistance through proper use of antibiotics is covered in Chapter 5.

PUBLIC HEALTH INITIATIVES

On May 5, 2009, President Obama asked Congress to approve and fund a new global health strategy that would cost $63 billion over six years. The plan would improve health care around the

world, especially infection control and prevention, and would focus mainly on AIDS. But money would also be used to combat TB, malaria, and other tropical diseases.

"In the twenty-first century, disease flows freely across borders and oceans . . . ," the president said. "We cannot wall ourselves off from the world and hope for the best, nor ignore the public health challenges beyond our borders."[1]

International organizations have joined the fight against infectious diseases. In 2001, the WHO introduced the first global plan for solving the critical health problems caused by antimicrobial drug resistance. The WHO Global Strategy for Containment of Antimicrobial Resistance includes plans for preventing disease, obtaining antimicrobial drugs and using them correctly, slowing the rate of drug resistance and tracking it (surveillance), and convincing governments to take immediate action and then giving them expert advice. More than 120 countries have received a Model List of Essential Medicines customized for their most urgent needs.[2]

Educating the public and medical professionals is a major part of preventing disease and is part of most public health initiatives.

One of the world's leading initiatives to eradicate TB, Stop TB, was created in 1998 by the WHO and several drug manufacturers. Stop TB's ultimate goal is eliminating the disease as a public health problem by 2050. The cornerstone of the Stop TB strategy is expansion of the Directly Observed Treatment, Short-course (DOTS) protocol to the remotest areas of the world.

What Is DOTS?

DOTS stands for Directly Observed Treatment, Short-course. It is an inexpensive, highly effective international protocol for treating TB patients that was developed by the World Health Organization in 1995. Patients are observed taking their TB medications to make sure they get the right dose at the right time, do not forget or skip doses, and do not hoard or sell their drugs. The person observing may be a medical professional at a clinic or a friend or family member at home.

For DOTS to work, several rules must be followed:

- Countries must make a financial commitment to follow the program.
- TB must be correctly diagnosed in high-quality labs, using improved bacteriology techniques.
- Each patient with TB must be registered.
- The drug supply must be reliable, and standardized multidrug treatment must be given. For maximum effect, patients must get the same TB medications throughout their treatment.
- Patient outcomes must be evaluated to see how effective the treatment is.

When followed correctly, DOTS is the most effective strategy for controlling TB worldwide. It can be used just as successfully in Africa as in New York City. More than 17.1 million patients were treated between 1995 and 2003, and 182 countries were using the protocol by the end of 2003. That year, 1.8 million new TB cases were reported, and 82 percent of people were successfully treated.[3]

The Stop TB program is attempting to eradicate tuberculosis and end the suffering this disease causes, such as for this three-generation family in Bangladesh.

The program addresses the growing problems of people with both TB and HIV/AIDS as well as those with MDR-TB. Stop TB also promotes TB research and strives to get people and communities involved in controlling TB.

Since 1998, progress has been close to expectations, with millions of patients diagnosed and treated successfully. The short-term goal of cutting prevalence and death rates in half compared to 1990 is expected to be reached by 2015, except in Africa and Eastern Europe.[4]

Some other TB health initiatives include TB Alliance, which seeks to discover better drugs for the treatment of non-drug-resistant TB that may also work against MDR-TB, and TB Free, which trains volunteers in South Africa to help patients stick to their six-month drug treatment. Two other initiatives are AERAS, a group that seeks new vaccines, and FIND, which works on new diagnostic tests. TB Alliance, AERAS, and FIND are all mainly funded by the Bill and Melinda Gates Foundation, which provides nearly as much money as WHO does for global health initiatives.

Public health initiatives are also in place for many other infectious diseases. The Malaria Vaccine Initiative works to speed up the development of malaria vaccines, and the Medicines for Malaria Venture supports the development of new anti-malarial drugs. The MRSA Leadership Initiative focuses on educating the medical community and the public about MRSA and halting its spread. In addition to U.S. government programs, dozens of other AIDS initiatives exist worldwide, including Tanzania Care, which trains medical professionals to fight AIDS in that country, and Secure the Future, which helps women and children affected by AIDS in sub-Saharan Africa.

Educating the public and medical professionals is a major part of preventing disease and is part of most public health initiatives. The CDC works with state and local health departments on public awareness campaigns to get the word out about how to recognize, prevent, and treat various infectious diseases. The 2009 H1N1 flu outbreak is a case in point. Besides providing up-to-date information on its Web site, the CDC developed and distributed influenza diagnostic kits to 350 labs in the United States and 130 other countries. The CDC also sent antiviral drugs, masks, and other protective equipment to all fifty states.[5]

VACCINES

In 1955, a national vaccination program was launched to combat polio, a crippling disease that had reached epidemic proportions in the United States. The Salk and Sabin vaccines caused polio rates to plummet from 35,000 cases in 1953 to only 121 cases by 1964. Now the disease has been eradicated in this country and almost everywhere else in the Western world.[6]

Parents and their children wait to enter a clinic to receive the polio vaccine in 1953. The vaccine has effectively eradicated the disease in the United States.

Unfortunately, vaccines have not yet been developed for every infectious disease. Among the diseases covered in this book, there are only vaccines for *S. pneumoniae* and influenza. A vaccine for H1N1 flu was introduced in October 2009, and vaccines for seasonal flu have been available since 1944. Vaccine research is ongoing for HIV, malaria, and other infections.

When vaccinations prevent disease, they also help prevent or slow down the development of drug resistance. Because people get sick less often and there are fewer cases of disease, doctors prescribe fewer antimicrobial drugs, and the number of drug-resistant bugs decreases.

Vaccination does more than protect individuals; it also protects whole populations. If everyone in a certain area is vaccinated (immunized) against a disease, the microbe causing the disease has a hard time finding someone to infect. When *almost* everyone is vaccinated against a certain disease, even those who are not vaccinated are protected because they have little chance of crossing paths with an infected person. This is called herd immunity.

TB Vaccine

The only vaccine for TB currently in use is the century-old Bacillus Calmette-Guérin, or BCG vaccine. The most widely used vaccine in the world, BCG has been given to more than 3 billion people, including newborn babies, especially in developing countries where the risk of early TB infection and death are high.[7] In South Africa, where TB rates are the highest in the world, the vaccine is given to all children under age three.

The BCG vaccine is thought to protect children from dying of uncontrolled and disseminated TB infection, but is ineffective against the most common form of disease among adults, pulmonary TB. Being vaccinated a second or third time does not increase protection.[8] The vaccine has never been used routinely in the United States, but there are a few exceptions. It may be given to infants and children who have been exposed to adults with TB. Health-care workers who care for MDR-TB patients or are in situations where TB control precautions were unsuccessful may also be vaccinated.

One controversy over the use of BCG is the fact that vaccinated people will always test positive on a TB skin test, as if they have been infected with TB. This makes it difficult to tell whether someone is actually infected and is one reason the vaccine is not used in this country.

BCG has been shown to be effective in protecting children from severe forms of TB that do not affect the lungs (extra-pulmonary TB). Unfortunately, pulmonary TB is the most prevalent type and the one that is in the most danger of becoming drug resistant and spreading to other people.

How Do Vaccines Work?

Vaccines enable the body to quickly fight off bacteria and other bugs that cause infection. Vaccinations are usually given by injection, but they may also be given by mouth or nasal spray. They always involve putting some kind of infectious agent, either a bacteria or a virus, into a person's body, but the organism is not strong enough to cause disease. The bacteria or virus may be weakened, killed, or altered. Sometimes only the parts of the germ that the immune system recognizes are in the vaccine.

When these weak or altered bacteria or viruses enter the body, the immune system produces specific antibodies against that microbe. Because the infectious agent is weak or even dead already, the antibodies can quickly overwhelm it. Later, if the person is exposed to a strong, active version of the organism, the immune system can immediately recognize it and has the antibodies to destroy it before disease develops.

Streptococcal Pneumonia Vaccine

In 2000, a vaccine for infants and children became available against S. pneumoniae, which causes pneumococcal pneumonia, otitis media (ear infections), and other diseases such as bacterial meningitis, all of which are invasive diseases. Called the pneumococcal conjugate vaccine, it reduced the rate of invasive pneumococcal disease in children under two by 70 to 80 percent between 1998 (just before the vaccine was licensed) and 2003.[9] Another S. pneumoniae vaccine is now available for adults over age sixty-five and other people with weakened immune systems, such as those with HIV. Experts hope that more widespread use of these vaccines, along with more sensible use of antibiotics, will slow or even reverse drug resistance.[10] Because children's vaccines are sometimes in short supply, and many adults do not bother to get vaccinated, about 6,000 Americans still die of invasive disease every year.[11]

H1N1 Flu Vaccine

When the H1N1 flu first appeared, researchers from several different drug manufacturers worked feverishly to make a vaccine. Their hard work paid off, and a vaccine became available in the fall of 2009. It does not offer protection against the seasonal flu and vice versa, so people needed to get two flu shots in the 2009–2010 flu season.

Those advised to get the H1N1 flu shot include children and young adults, pregnant women, health-care workers, and people with health conditions that weaken their immune systems. Seasonal flu vaccines are usually available every September and are given throughout the fall and early winter in preparation for peak flu season in January. They are available in shots (a killed virus) or nasal sprays (a weakened live virus). People over age fifty, those with weakened immune systems, pregnant women, children aged six months to nineteen years, and health-care workers are advised to get vaccinated against seasonal flu. But many other people also get vaccinated to avoid catching the flu.

A boy receives the H1N1 vaccine in November 2009. The CDC included children and young adults among those recommended to receive the H1N1 vaccine.

TRAVEL PRECAUTIONS AGAINST SUPERBUGS

People are traveling more than ever today, and some are choosing exotic locations. About eight weeks before traveling, especially to developing countries, people should check with their doctors to see what vaccinations are required. Going to the doctor far in advance ensures that vaccines have time to become effective. Some vaccinations also have to be given in a series, over a period of days or weeks.

The CDC divides travel vaccines into three categories: routine, recommended, and required. Routine vaccinations are those like a tetanus shot that you regularly get in the United States. Recommended vaccines depend on your destination. The only two required vaccines are the yellow fever vaccine (for sub-Saharan Africa) and a meningococcal vaccination (for Saudi Arabia). The CDC Web site lists all vaccinations in these three categories alphabetically by country. The site also includes other preventive measures for each destination, such as bed nets and insect repellant for countries where malaria is prevalent.

IMMIGRATION SCREENING FOR SUPERBUGS

Requirements also exist for traveling into the United States. To prevent people with infectious diseases, including drug-resistant TB and other drug-resistant infections, from entering the country, refugees and immigrants must have a medical examination before they can obtain a visa. The CDC regulates overseas medical examinations and establishes guidelines. Examinations are performed by doctors designated by the U.S. Department of State.

The examinations identify people with serious mental or physical health problems, especially infectious diseases. People who are not granted visas include not only those with infections but also drug addicts or abusers, people with untreated sexually transmitted diseases, and people with HIV or active TB. People with latent TB are granted visas.

New guidelines were established in 2007 for TB screening outside the United States and treatment for people with active TB who are seeking visas. Before a TB patient comes to the United States, he or she must have chest X-rays and sputum cultures as well as drug susceptibility tests to see what drugs will work best for the patient. In addition, TB patients must begin DOTS therapy before traveling to the United States.

IMPORTANCE OF HAND WASHING

Catching an infectious disease is often a matter of luck, or rather, *bad* luck. A person may be in the wrong place at the wrong time, for example, sharing an elevator with someone who has an active TB infection who coughs or sneezes. But although luck plays a part, people can actually take many precautions to keep from contracting or passing on infectious diseases. A lot of these are just good hygiene or plain common sense.

The Clean Hands Campaign urges people to avoid spreading germs by washing their hands.

Mothers are right when they tell children to cover their mouth when coughing or to wash their hands after using the bathroom. Simple health practices can do a lot to prevent complicated diseases. The CDC calls hand washing one of the most important ways to avoid getting sick and reduce the spread of infection. Unclean hands spread all kinds of infections, including germs that have become resistant to antibiotics. Germs can also live for several hours on phones, computer keyboards, doorknobs, and a million other places. When you touch your dirty hands to your mouth, eyes, nose, or an open wound, you transmit the germs into your body.

Hand washing is so important, the CDC, the Canadian Centre for Occupational Health and Safety, the American Society for Microbiology, and other organizations have published pamphlets, posted instructions on their Web sites, and even made videos explaining why, when, and how to wash your hands. It may seem odd explaining something this simple, but the fact is, people do not wash their hands enough, and a recent survey proves it.

In a 2007 study by the American Society for Microbiology and the Soap and Detergent Association, 1,001 adult Americans were interviewed on the phone about their hand-washing habits. Nine out of ten said they always washed their hands after using a public restroom. To see if this was true, investigators discretely observed the hand-washing behavior of 6,076 adults in public restrooms in Atlanta, Chicago, New York City, and San Francisco. They found that only three out of four people (about 77 percent) washed their

Hand Washing 101

Everybody knows how to wash their hands, right? Wrong. Here is a short refresher course.

When to wash your hands:

- When they look dirty
- After going to the bathroom
- After changing diapers
- After blowing your nose or coughing or sneezing into your hand
- Before and after eating (including snacks)
- Before, during, and after preparing food (especially raw meat)
- Before putting in or taking out contact lenses
- After petting an animal or cleaning up animal waste
- Before and after taking care of someone who is sick or more than usual if someone in your house is sick.

You should always wash your hands after certain activities, including touching animals.

How to wash hands:

- Wet your hands thoroughly with warm running water.
- Lather them with soap and wash for fifteen to twenty seconds.
- Wash the front and back of your hands, wrists, palms, between your fingers, and under your fingernails. If you are wearing rings, wash them, and under them, as well.
- Rinse with warm water.
- Dry thoroughly with a clean cloth or paper towel.
- Use hand sanitizers when soap and water are not available.

Soap and water do not actually kill microbes. Instead, the combination makes hands and other surfaces slippery so the bugs "slide off." However, antibacterial soaps for cleaning hands and surfaces are not necessary, except in some hospital settings. In fact, overuse of antibacterial soaps may lead to the evolution of more bacteria with drug resistance.

hands, and women washed more than men. The exact numbers were: 2,038 male washers and 1,027 male non-washers, and 2,647 female washers and 364 female non-washers. Clearly, people overestimate the amount they wash or are simply too embarrassed to admit that they do not.[12]

Unclean hands spread all kinds of infections, including germs that have become resistant to antibiotics. Germs can also live for several hours on phones, computer keyboards, doorknobs, and a million other places.

GETTING SAVVY ABOUT SICKNESS

What can individuals do to keep from getting or spreading infections? They can learn as much as possible about the diseases they have and the ones they do not want to catch.

Preventing TB

People who know they are infected with TB can try hard to keep from spreading it, and people who are around them can take precautions, too. To keep from spreading TB, patients should take all their medicine, keep their doctor's appointments, and tell their doctor the names of people they have been in close contact with. They should stay home from work or school and not travel until their doctor confirms they are no longer contagious. As long as they have TB, people should avoid close contact with others, and cover their noses and mouths when they cough or sneeze. They should wash their hands often, get plenty of sleep, eat well, and exercise. Good health habits will speed their recovery by helping them avoid other infections and maintaining a good immune system.

Smoking Causes TB

Smoking does not cause TB on its own. But along with other factors, it does greatly increase the chance of getting TB. In 2007, researchers Michael Bates and Kirk Smith at the University of California, Berkeley, analyzed twenty-four separate studies on smoking and TB. Putting all these research findings together, they concluded that smokers have a 73 percent greater chance of becoming infected with TB than nonsmokers. Smokers who already have TB infection are about 50 percent more likely to develop active TB disease than nonsmokers in the same population. On the whole, a smoker has about a 2.5 times greater risk of developing active TB than a nonsmoker.

"Because it increases the number of active TB cases, we estimate that smoking is related to half a million of the 1.7 million TB deaths a year," Smith said.

"Currently, smoking cessation is not a part of TB control programs," said Bates. "The evidence from this study suggests that it should be."[13]

People living with someone who has TB should avoid close contact, if possible, especially if the patient has a cough. They should open windows to keep the air circulating, to avoid breathing stale air filled with germs. Family, friends, and others in regular contact should consult with a doctor because they may need to be tested for TB.

Preventing MRSA

To prevent MRSA, take these precautions:

- Wash your hands often, especially after being in a public place.
- Keep cuts clean and covered with a bandage until healed. Dispose of used bandages in a sealed plastic bag if at all possible.
- Do not touch other people's cuts or bandages.

- Do not share towels, razors, or other personal items.
- Because MRSA can stay alive for hours to months on surfaces, take precautions in the gym or locker room. Clean weight benches with a disinfectant before lying or sitting on them, and do not sit on locker room benches without putting a towel down first.
- Shower immediately after athletic games or practices and wash gym clothes after every wearing.
- If a cut is draining, swollen, or red (signs of infection), visit a doctor and ask if you need a MRSA test. Do not participate in sports or go to the gym until the cut is healed.
- Follow your doctor's orders when taking antibiotics. Contact the doctor if the infection has not improved in a few days.

Preventing Streptococcal Pneumonia

The first line of defense against *S. pneumoniae* is to get vaccinated. Two separate vaccines are available: one for children that helps prevent ear infections and pneumonia, and another for people over age sixty-five, children over age two, and adults with diseases that weaken their immune systems. The pneumococcal conjugate vaccine for children is given several times between infancy and age two and is mandatory in the United States and several other countries. The 23-valent polysaccharide vaccine for adults is recommended, but not mandatory.

S. *pneumoniae* is spread through respiratory droplets, so people who become infected should cover their mouths and noses when coughing and sneezing and wash their hands often.

Preventing Gram-Negative Bacterial Infections

Almost all gram-negative bacterial infections have occurred in hospital settings. The best way to keep from spreading them is by hand washing. Health-care workers must wash their hands before entering patients' rooms and follow other infection-control techniques, including disinfecting counters, beds, curtains between beds, and other parts of the hospital environment.

Visitors should wash their clothes when they get home from the hospital. Women should not set their purses on the floor where they can pick up bacteria. And of course, everyone should wash their hands before entering a patient's room, although they should not use bar soap in any hospital bathroom.

Studies in Europe, Canada, and the United States have shown that an alarming percentage of doctors and nurses do not wash their hands between patients. They may be in a rush and simply forget, or figure it is not necessary because it was only a quick visit and they did not touch anything. But with the upsurge in hospital-acquired infections, many hospitals are launching infection-control campaigns that emphasize hand washing.

One example is a program that took place at Cedars-Sinai Medical Center in Los Angeles. The hospital wanted to make infection-control second nature to employees and appointed a "Hand Hygiene Safety Posse" to observe whether staff members washed their hands. Dispensers with antiseptic cleanser were put all over the hospital, including in patient rooms, visitor waiting areas, and hallways. Hospital officials said the program, complete with posters declaring, "The power is in your hands. Please help us protect our patients' health," also encouraged patients and visitors to speak up if they noticed any staff forgetting to wash.[14]

Preventing Malaria

Eradicating malaria is not a realistic goal in countries where the disease flourishes. Controlling it is the goal. This is achieved through case management (diagnosis and treatment of patients who have malaria), vector (insect) control, and disease prevention through distribution of antimalarial drugs.

Case management: People who have malaria should be treated within twenty-four hours of getting symptoms. Quick treatment kills the malaria parasite before it can be transmitted to other people via insect bites. It also reduces the severity of the disease in the infected person.

HOW REAL PEOPLE DEAL: A VISIT TO GHANA GONE WRONG

Harry Yirrell thought he was immune to malaria, and it cost him his life.

After high school in England, Harry decided to spend four months as a volunteer in a small village in Ghana, Africa. Before he left, he rushed around, buying supplies and getting the necessary inoculations and drugs for malaria and other diseases.

Harry loved Africa. He helped build a new school, taught the children to read and play rugby, and shared his love of music. Known for his generosity, he even sold his mobile phone to buy furniture for the school. Then he made a fatal mistake: He gave some villagers his malaria medicine.

Harry Yirrell died of malaria at the age of twenty. He had given away his malaria pills while volunteering in Africa in 2005.

When Harry returned home, he looked strong, tanned, and healthy. His parents were shocked when he told them he had given his malaria medicine away and had not used insect repellant. "I don't get malaria," he joked.

A week after he got home, Harry developed a headache and fatigue, which he blamed on too much partying with friends. But then he developed a high fever, sweating, chills, and an excruciating pain in his head. He was admitted to the hospital, where blood tests showed he had malaria.

Harry was put on intravenous antibiotics and seemed to be getting better. The doctor expected him to make a full recovery. But after two days, he started having trouble breathing and was placed on a ventilator. The malaria had caused his lungs to fill with fluid. Because his body was not getting enough oxygen, his organs shut down. Everyone was shocked when Harry died.

His parents and three brothers were devastated. They knew Harry was very ill, but they never believed he would die. They did not realize that although malaria can be cured, it must be diagnosed and treated immediately. By the time Harry got home from Africa, it was probably already too late.

After Harry's death, his mother Jo became an ambassador for the charity Malaria No More. When she visited the village in Ghana where Harry had worked, she met other mothers who had lost their children to malaria.

"My life's work is now to raise awareness and to raise money," Jo said. "A child dies of malaria every thirty seconds in Africa."[15]

Vector control: The mosquito is the vector, or carrier, of malaria. Controlling the number of mosquitoes or reducing the contact between mosquitoes and humans reduces the number of disease-causing bites. Some large-scale methods include spraying insecticides inside houses and destroying mosquito breeding sites, but money is not always available for this in poor countries.

Individual measures include sleeping with insecticide-treated bed nets, wearing protective clothing, applying insect repellant, and staying indoors between dusk and dawn, when the most mosquitoes are out.

Disease prevention: Antimalarial drugs do not prevent infection, but they can kill the parasite once it gets into the blood. These drugs are only given to especially vulnerable people in countries with a risk of malaria, such as pregnant women and infants. The drugs are also given to people traveling to these countries.

Because malaria currently occurs mainly in impoverished countries, controlling it is hindered by lack of money for drugs, lack of understanding about the disease, and lack of adequate health care and facilities. Drug resistance is also a stumbling block. Malaria parasites are becoming resistant to antimalarial drugs, and alternate drugs are more expensive and not as safe. The mosquitoes that carry the parasites are also becoming resistant to the insecticides used to control them.

Preventing HIV/AIDS

AIDS is not transmitted by casual contact or living in a household with an infected person. It is transmitted sexually, through shared needles, or during pregnancy, childbirth, or breastfeeding. Knowledge is the best medicine. People should get tested for the disease, and regardless of whether they have it, use a condom every time they have sex.

Prevention of co-infection of HIV and TB is mainly a screening effort. The CDC recommends that all people who are HIV-positive have TB tests. If they have latent TB, they can then receive drugs to prevent active disease. If they have active TB, they can get treatment and counseling. Conversely, people with TB should be tested for HIV so they can get treatment and counseling, if necessary.

The CDC recommends that all people who are HIV-positive have TB tests.

Preventing Influenza

Getting vaccinated is the best way to avoid getting the flu. Two antiviral drugs—oseltamivir (Tamiflu) and zanamivir (Relenza) are also available. They help reduce the severity of flu in people who have been exposed. The first drug is for people over age one, and the second is for people over age seven.

During flu season, people should avoid touching their eyes, nose, or mouth and wash their hands often, especially if someone in their household is infected. At work, disinfecting phones, computer keyboards, and other equipment used by many people may help cut infections. People who have the flu should stay home from school or work until twenty-four hours after their symptoms go away.

CHAPTER FIVE

Testing and Treatment

We have come a long way since the discovery of antibiotics, vaccines, and other "miracle drugs" to fight infection. In the early twentieth century and before, it really was a miracle if a person survived TB or another infectious disease. Actually, they were lucky if they survived the *treatments*, which for TB ranged from sleeping outside in the winter to Monsieur Crotte's electrical cure, in which patients were given electrical shocks to the chest.[1]

Tuberculosis, malaria, HIV, and other drug-resistant infections remain a global scourge in part because proper diagnosis and treatment requires stamina and resources that people—both patients and providers—are not always able to muster. And wherever we fail, the disease succeeds.

DIAGNOSING TB

When a person visits a doctor's office complaining of a cough lasting more than three weeks, coughing up blood, or chest pain, a doctor will probably suspect a TB infection. The first steps in diagnosing the disease are the medical history and physical examination.

During the medical history, the doctor asks questions to assess the patient's risk factors for TB. For example, does anyone in the household have TB? Did the patient recently immigrate from another country? Has the person traveled to another country recently? Is HIV or another infection that weakens the immune system present?

The Mantoux Test

Robert Koch's vaccine for TB, composed of tuberculin—dead, concentrated *M. tuberculosis*—did not turn out to be a shield against the disease. But the would-be vaccine was put to good use in 1907, when French physician Charles Mantoux used it in a skin test for TB. This test was able to show whether a person had ever been infected with TB.

The Mantoux or skin test for TB is typically given at a doctor's office or clinic. The test is quick and relatively painless. It consists of inserting a small needle just below the skin on the underside of the forearm and injecting a small amount of tuberculin, called purified protein derivative (PPD). A few days later, the person returns to the doctor's office to have the injection site examined for a reaction.

If nothing happens, this is called a negative reaction, and the person probably is not infected with TB. But if someone has been infected, the immune system remembers and attacks the injected tuberculin, just as if live bacteria were invading. This causes a hard, red bump to appear at the injection site forty-eight to seventy-two hours later. However, this positive reaction does not show whether the TB is active.

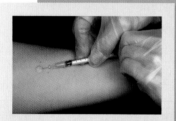

The Mantoux test is given to determine whether a patient has tuberculosis, though it cannot show whether the TB is active and it sometimes gives false positive test results.

Although the skin test is a useful diagnostic tool, it has several drawbacks. People may think they have TB when they do not (false positive test results) or they may have TB, but the test does not show it (false negative results).

False negative results can occur in people who have recently become infected with TB. Because the bacteria grow so slowly, there may not be enough of them in the body for the immune system to react to the tuberculin. On the other hand, the immune system may not even try to mount a defense in people with severely weakened immune systems or overwhelming TB infection.

False positive results may occur when someone has been infected, not with TB, but with a bacterium that is similar to the one that causes TB. In addition, people who have recently received the BCG vaccine will also have false positive results.

During the physical examination, the doctor listens to the patient's lungs with a stethoscope, checking for abnormal breathing sounds. The doctor also checks for signs of extrapulmonary TB, such as swollen lymph nodes.

If the doctor suspects TB, he or she will then order several tests. Common tests include a Mantoux (skin) test, a chest X-ray, and a sputum sample. The Mantoux test is the most frequently used screening tool for the disease but it only shows if someone has ever been infected with TB bacteria—the infection may not be active. If this test is positive, a sputum sample and chest X-ray are performed to see if active TB is present. Test results, combined with the history and physical exam, allow the doctor to make an accurate diagnosis.

Chest X-Ray

The X-ray was invented in 1895 by German physicist Wilhelm Roentgen, but it was not widely used in medicine until the 1930s. Back then, large numbers of people were given X-rays to screen for TB. Today, X-rays are used more cautiously, because we now know that having too many increases the risk of cancer.

The chest X-ray is a necessary tool for diagnosing active TB. This painless test is done in a doctor's office, clinic, or hospital. People must remove their clothes from the waist up, put on a hospital gown, and remove eyeglasses and jewelry. Then they stand in front of the X-ray machine. X-rays are usually taken from the back and side. Patients must not move or breathe for a few seconds while the image is being taken.

A chest X-ray will help diagnose an active or latent TB infection by showing lung abnormalities. White spots show where the immune system has walled off TB bacteria and indicate a latent infection. Nodules, scars, and cavities may be caused by active TB. The X-ray will also show how much damage the infection has caused.

Laboratory Tests

If a skin test and chest X-ray are positive, the doctor will usually order laboratory tests to confirm the diagnosis of TB and see what drugs will be most effective. In the meantime, the patient will be started on antibiotics. The most common lab test is a sputum test, but a blood test is occasionally done as well. To test for extrapulmonary TB, the doctor may take samples of fluids from other areas, such as from the brain and spinal cord if TB meningitis is suspected.

Sputum test: When someone with active TB coughs, the sputum they eject from their lungs into the air contains TB bacteria. Sputum tests have been a cornerstone of identifying active TB disease for a century and are the most common TB testing method worldwide.

A sputum test is also called a sputum stain, TB smear, or acid-fast bacilli stain. It starts with a coughed-up sputum sample, which the patient collects at home. This is not the same as spitting out saliva—sputum comes from deep inside the lungs. Collecting the sample correctly is very important, and patients are given instructions on how to do this.

Once the doctor has the sample, it goes to a lab for analysis. There, it is smeared on a slide, stained with dyes, and examined under a microscope for the presence of TB bacteria. False positive results may occur because the dyes react to other types of bacteria besides those that cause TB. False negative results may occur if the number of TB bacteria are too low to show up with staining. To be sure the person has a TB infection and not something else, the specimen may be cultured to encourage bacterial growth.

Bacteria in sputum cultures are also tested for resistance to commonly used TB drugs. This helps doctors know what medicines to prescribe. One major drawback to sputum cultures is the fact that TB bacteria grow so slowly that test results can take from two to eight weeks. Testing the cultures for effective antibiotics can take even longer. This is unfortunate, because

Collecting a Sputum Sample

Have you heard the one about the guy who stayed up all night studying for his urine test? Preparing a sample of phlegm for a sputum test sounds like a joke, too, but it is actually serious business, and doing it right is very important. Otherwise, the test results will not be accurate. When a doctor orders a sputum sample, the patient goes home with a sterile plastic tube that fits inside a metal container and the following instructions:

- Sputum from the lungs is thick and sticky. It does not include saliva, which is thin and watery. Sputum must be coughed up from deep in the lungs.
- Do not open the tube until you are ready to use it, and do not touch the inside.
- Collect sputum on waking in the morning.
- Go outside or at least open a window so others are not exposed to TB germs.
- Take a deep breath and hold it for five seconds. Breathe out slowly. Then take another deep breath and cough hard until sputum comes up into the throat.
- Spit the sputum into the tube. Repeat these steps until the sputum reaches the five-milliliter mark on the tube.
- Screw the cap on the tube tightly, wipe off the outside with a tissue, and put the tube in the metal container and screw the lid on tightly.
- Put the container in the refrigerator if the test cannot be brought to the doctor's office immediately. Do not store it at room temperature or in the freezer.[2]

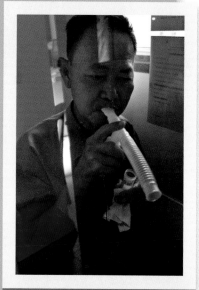

Pich Chhieng takes a sputum test at a California medical center to determine whether he still has tuberculosis. He was infected in Cambodia and traveled to the United States with TB in 2006.

even though doctors prescribe antibiotics right away, they may not be the ones the patient needs. Effective TB treatment needs to be started as soon as possible to prevent further lung damage and keep people from spreading the infection to others.

Other tests: A newer test called the microscopic-observation drug-susceptibility (MODS) assay spots TB bacteria in sputum in only seven days. It can also identify drug-resistant strains of bacteria. This simple test costs only $3 per person and is mainly used in developing countries.[3]

The high-tech polymerase chain reaction (PCR) test takes a piece of DNA (the chemical carrying hereditary information) from the TB bacterium and replicates it millions of times. The test is so sensitive that it can pinpoint TB bacteria in one infected lung cell amid thousands of uninfected ones. Unfortunately, the test is too expensive to be used routinely.

A blood test called the interferon gamma release assay (IGRA) was developed in 2005. Blood is drawn from a patient and then mixed with synthetic TB proteins in a lab. If an immune response is noted under a microscope, the patient has been infected with TB bacteria. This test is more rapid than the Mantoux test because results are available in only twenty-four hours without a return to the doctor's office to inspect the test site, and having had the BCG vaccine does not affect results. However, the test is still relatively new, so it is not yet widely available.

TREATING TB

In a perfect world, patients would be diagnosed quickly, start treatment immediately, and be cured in a few weeks. But what actually happens is that diagnosing TB takes weeks, people wait a long time to get their antibiotics, and then they wait and wait and wait to be cured.

It usually takes at least six to nine months to destroy the TB bacteria. The length of treatment is affected by the patient's age and general health, whether the disease is latent or active,

What Is a Culture?

Cultures are laboratory tests performed to see what microorganisms are responsible for infections. When testing for TB, MRSA, or other infections, tissue or body fluid specimens are placed in a substance called a medium that encourages their microbial growth. Bacterial cultures are performed by spreading the specimen on several culture plates and then putting them in a container called an incubator at human body temperature for one to two days. Any bacteria present will multiply, and become visible and identifiable under a microscope. Viral cultures are grown by mixing the specimen in a test tube with commercially prepared animal cells. If a virus is present, it causes the animal cells to change in certain ways that can be seen under a microscope. Some viruses and bacteria take several days or even several weeks to grow.

and whether the TB is drug resistant. Patients must take their medicine exactly as the doctor orders, for as long as ordered. Using the DOTS protocol, during which someone observes patients taking their drugs, is recommended for all patients.

Treating Latent and Active TB

The goal of treating latent TB is killing the bacteria before it turns into active disease. Once active TB has been ruled out, the usual treatment for latent TB is isoniazid or rifampin for six to nine months. People with latent TB are not contagious, so they can continue their normal activities during treatment.

The treatment for active TB is a combination of four drugs: isoniazid, rifampin, pyrazinamide, and ethambutol. The first three drugs may be combined into one pill, which makes treatment easier. In less severe cases, one or two drugs might be discontinued after a few months. Patients are often isolated in the hospital for the first two weeks or until tests show they are no longer contagious. Afterward, they will be isolated at home and warned not to leave unless they have a doctor's appointment. They will not be allowed visitors.

Serious side effects of anti-TB drugs occasionally occur. Hepatitis, a life-threatening liver disease, is possible, so patients need careful monitoring. During treatment, patients should avoid drinking alcohol and taking Tylenol and other medicines containing acetaminophen, because both increase the chance of liver damage. Other side effects include stomach upset, nausea and vomiting, loss of appetite, and fever. These side effects usually go away, but patients should report them to their doctors. They should *not* get discouraged and stop taking their medicine! Especially in developing countries, some patients feel that their side effects make it difficult for them to work to feed their families and themselves. They may quit the medication to earn money to eat, but eventually their untreated TB will make working impossible as they get sicker and sicker and eventually die.

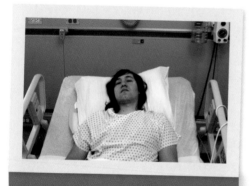

Patients who may have active TB are often kept in the hospital for the first two weeks of treatment until doctors have determined that they are no longer contagious.

To monitor the effectiveness of treatment, patients need sputum cultures at least once a month until two consecutive tests come back negative. They should also have monthly checkups to make sure they are taking their drugs correctly and to check for side effects. Complying with the treatment regimen is definitely worth it— the cure rate for TB that is not drug resistant is at least 95 percent![4]

Treating Drug-Resistant TB

Multidrug-resistant TB (MDR-TB) bacteria are resistant to both isoniazid and rifampin, which are the most often prescribed first-line drugs for TB. More than 500,000 cases of MDR-TB occur every year worldwide, in more than 50 countries.[5] These figures are probably lower than the actual extent because drug susceptibility tests are limited in developing countries. Treatment of MDR-TB can be extremely complicated, taking up to two years. It can also be very expensive, costing up to one hundred times more than other drugs. But inappropriate or inadequate treatment can have deadly consequences.[6]

Patients are tested for drug-resistant bacteria with a sputum culture. While they wait weeks for results, they are started on several drugs. Once drug resistance is verified, the drugs and dosages are adjusted. Drugs other than isoniazid and rifampin are called second-line drugs, and include ethionamide, para-aminosalicylic acid, cycloserine, ciprofloxacin, ofloxacin, amikacin, capreomycin, kanamycin, and clofazimine. The last three drugs can only be given by injection. Some of these are highly toxic, and include side effects ranging from dizziness and upset stomach to convulsions, hearing loss, and organ damage. Even when treatment is followed precisely, the success rate is only 60 to 70 percent, and sometimes surgery is necessary.[7] A lobectomy may be performed to remove the affected lobes of the lung, as long as only one or two lobes are infected with TB.

Some patients with drug-resistant TB require special consideration. Those co-infected with HIV need the usual TB drugs, but because they are also taking many HIV drugs, they need to be monitored extra carefully to make sure the drugs do not interact in harmful ways. Children with drug-resistant TB can take most of the drugs adults can, but they should be under the care of a pediatric TB specialist. Pregnant women with drug-resistant TB must also work with specialists because most drugs for MDR-TB can harm the fetus. In addition, people in close contact with those who have drug-resistant TB should take medicine to prevent getting infected themselves.

The most deadly type of TB is XDR-TB, which is resistant to the first-line drugs isoniazid and rifampin as well as several second-line drugs. An estimated 40,000 cases emerge annually, and as of 2008, they were found in 45 countries.[8] Like MDR-TB, XDR-TB is very likely underreported in certain parts of the developing world. It is known to be spreading and gaining a foothold in places like sub-Saharan Africa. In 2006, fifty-three patients with XDR-TB were found in a rural town in South Africa, all of whom were also infected with HIV, and fifty-two people died within fifty-one days of being diagnosed.[9] However, in countries with good TB control programs, up to 60 percent of people with XDR-TB can be cured.[10] Treatment is a "cocktail" of four or more drugs taken for eighteen months to two years or even longer.

The most deadly type of TB is XDR-TB, which is resistant to the first-line drugs isoniazid and rifampin as well as several second-line drugs.

Treating TB/HIV

Statistics reveal the global dimensions of TB/HIV:

- Forty million people are living with HIV/AIDS, and one-third of them are co-infected with TB.
- People who are HIV-positive make up 7.6 percent of all TB cases.
- Only 3 percent of TB patients are tested for HIV.
- People with HIV are up to fifty times more likely to develop TB in their lifetime than those who are HIV negative.
- TB patients rarely get treated for HIV. In 2003, only 1,349 co-infected people in the world reportedly took HIV drugs.[11]

The bottom line? Everyone with HIV should be tested for TB. Because HIV/AIDS severely weakens the immune system, people with this disease are highly susceptible to other infections, like TB. They are also more apt to get active TB because their bodies are not strong enough to ward off the bacteria.

Without treatment, people living with both HIV and TB often die in a few months.

Drug interactions: Even when people get treated, problems arise. The powerful antiretroviral drugs used to treat HIV/AIDS interact with equally powerful TB drugs. Drugs for both diseases can damage kidneys, so taking them together increases this risk. The TB drug rifampin can cause blood levels of certain HIV drugs (protease inhibitors and nonnucleoside reverse transcriptase inhibitors) to drop so much they stop controlling the virus. On the other hand, HIV drugs can raise blood levels of TB drugs, increasing the drugs' side effects.

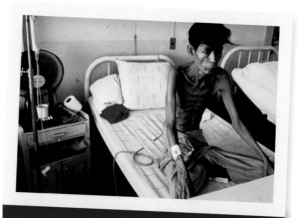

This TB patient in Thailand is co-infected with HIV. He has lost half of his original body weight due to both the ravages of the diseases and the harsh effects of drug treatment.

For these reasons, doctors may have patients stop HIV/AIDS drugs until they finish a short course of TB drugs, including rifampin. Sometimes another TB drug may be substituted for rifampin. In either case, patients on dual therapy should be monitored closely by an expert in both diseases. Treatment with TB drugs usually lasts six to nine months.

Drug-resistance: In 2008, the World Health Organization reported that MDR-TB was almost twice as common in TB/HIV patients as in those without HIV. Unfortunately, the true extent of the problem is still unknown because many African countries lack the equipment and trained people to identify drug-resistant TB. Africa has the highest incidence of both TB and HIV/AIDS in the world.[12]

DIAGNOSING AND TREATING OTHER SUPERBUGS

Other infections caused by bacteria, as well as those caused by parasites and viruses, also need prompt diagnosis and treatment. Patients visiting a doctor or clinic will go through a history and physical examination process similar to one they would undergo if they were suspected to have TB. Then, depending on the doctor's findings, tests will usually be ordered to help diagnose the infection and plan appropriate treatment.

MRSA

An *S. aureus* (staph) infection of the skin can be uncomplicated and treatable with common antibiotics. Or, it can turn out to be a potentially deadly strain of staph that is drug resistant, like MRSA. To be on the safe side, the CDC advises doctors to consider MRSA as a diagnosis whenever a patient has a serious skin infection.[13]

The doctor will ask if the patient works in a hospital or was recently hospitalized, has recently taken antibiotics, or if the patient has diabetes, HIV, or another disease that weakens the immune system. These are all risk factors for a staph infection. Also, if the patient has been around someone with MRSA or has already had this infection, there is an excellent chance the current staph infection is MRSA.

The doctor examines the skin infection and makes an educated guess about what is causing it. A staph infection can start out looking like a pimple or boil and then get red, swollen, warm, and painful, fill with pus or fluid, and develop a yellow or white center and a central point or head. In these cases, the doctor usually performs an incision and drainage, making a small cut in the infected area and allowing the fluid or pus to drain. He or she then disinfects the wound and covers it with gauze. This procedure helps the tissue heal more quickly. Patients may also be prescribed antibiotic soaps and ointments to use on affected areas. This may be all that is needed to cure a mild MRSA infection.[14]

If the patient has a fever and looks and feels sick, this suggests a more severe infection that might enter the bloodstream, where it can cause potentially deadly infections of the heart, brain, and lungs. In these cases, the doctor will order culture and sensitivity tests. The infected skin area will be swabbed and specimens sent to a lab for culturing. The first culture determines what bacterium is actually causing the infection—is it MRSA?

The second culture determines if the bacteria are resistant to any antibiotics. This is done by combining bacteria from the infected area with different antibiotics to see how well each drug stops the bacteria from growing. If the cause of the infection is staph, and the bacteria are resistant to first-line drugs in the penicillin family, the patient has MRSA. If no drug resistance is noted, the patient has a regular staph infection that can be treated with common antibiotics.

Usually, it takes twenty-four to seventy-two hours to get test results. In the meantime, patients may be given first- or second-line antibiotics to prevent the staph bacteria from getting worse and invading the bloodstream, where they can cause life-threatening illness. A new, faster method of MRSA screening, the polymerase chain reaction test, gives results in only an hour, but this test is expensive and still not widely used. It tests for the mecA gene in bacteria samples, which is the gene that makes the bacteria resistant to antibiotics.

Treatment for MRSA includes trimethoprim/sulfamethoxazole, minocyline, doxycycline, oxacillin, or tetracycline. Taking antibiotics exactly as prescribed until all the pills are gone is extremely important. Patients will also be sent home with instructions on how to care for their skin infection and how to prevent spreading it to others. These include keeping the wound covered with clean, dry bandages, washing their hands often, and washing sheets and personal items in hot water and laundry detergent.

Patients with more serious infections or who do not respond to initial treatment may be hospitalized, isolated in a private room, and given antibiotics intravenously. Serious MRSA infections are treated with vancomycin, linezolid, or daptomycin.

A staph infection can start out looking like a pimple or boil and then get red, swollen, warm, and painful, fill with pus or fluid, and develop a yellow or white center and a central point or head.

Streptococcal Pneumonia

Because *S. pneumoniae* causes several different infections, such as pneumonia, ear infections, and meningitis, patients may come to a doctor's office with a number of symptoms. When making a diagnosis, the doctor will consider the symptoms as well as the patient's age (the infection is more common in children and the elderly), whether another disease exists that weakens the immune system, and whether the patient has recently traveled to another country.

The doctor will usually order a complete blood count (CBC), and may order a spinal tap, sputum culture, and chest X-ray. When meningitis is suspected, a spinal tap is performed. Cerebrospinal fluid is withdrawn from the lower spinal canal with a thin needle and then tested.

Blood tests do not help diagnose pneumonia because these patients rarely have measurable levels of bacteria in their blood. A sputum culture showing *S. pneumoniae* bacteria suggests the disease. A chest X-ray showing firm, solid, fluid-filled lungs indicates pneumococcal pneumonia. So does a high white blood cell count.

Once a diagnosis is made, the bacteria are tested for drug resistance using a sensitivity test. Results can take up to seventy-two hours, so antibiotics are administered in the interim.

HOW REAL PEOPLE DEAL: MRSA STRIKES A TODDLER

Hannah Thompson was in motion from the time she woke up until her parents, Gala and Brian, forced her to go to bed. So when the energetic two-year-old suddenly started limping, then refused to even stand on her own, her parents knew something was seriously wrong.

They took her to the doctor, who ordered several tests, including a spinal tap, a bone scan, and a CT scan. But the results all came back normal. Then Hannah stopped eating and drinking and developed a high fever. The doctor admitted her to the hospital.

Because she had a high fever, the doctors suspected Hannah had some kind of infection and ordered blood tests. The tests revealed methicillin-resistant *Staphylococcus aureus* (MRSA), a type of bacterial infection that common antibiotics like penicillin cannot cure. If it is not treated promptly, it can damage organs and have lethal consequences. Luckily, the doctors caught the infection in time and gave Hannah stronger antibiotics. She started to get better almost immediately, and went home five days later.

The doctors still are not sure how Hannah got MRSA or where the infection started. She had a mark on her ankle that looked like a bite and a boil that her parents thought was diaper rash. They think the bacteria probably entered her body in one of those two places.

Now her parents are vigilant about keeping Hannah from getting another infection. They scrub her toys with a bleach solution and do not allow her and her five-year-old sister, Madeline, to share towels or bedding. They clean and cover cuts and scrapes immediately.

Doctors diagnosed two-year-old Hannah Thompson with MRSA after she developed symptoms that included high fever and lack of appetite.

"We feel like we dodged a bullet," Gala said.[15]

When test results are in, the doctor selects the antibiotics that will work best.

Penicillin is usually used to treat pneumococcal infections, but many strains of *S. pneumoniae* are becoming resistant to all drugs in this class of antibiotics, making treatment much more challenging. Alternate antibiotics include vancomycin, ceftriaxone, cefalaxime, and drugs in the fluoroquinolones class. But as with all second-line antibiotics, these drugs are more expensive, can have more serious side effects, and often have to be given intravenously.

Gram-Negative Bacterial Diseases

Gram-negative bacterial infections occur almost entirely in hospitals, but experts fear they are on the brink of spreading into the community. If a patient has characteristic symptoms—such as a high fever, chills, flulike symptoms, or a wound that drains pus—the doctor will obtain a culture. Typical culture locations include surgical wounds and IV insertion sites. Sputum, urine, and blood samples may also be obtained. In the lab, the harmful bacteria are identified, then tested for drug susceptibility. Because these tests take two or three days to complete, the doctor may start antibiotics and switch them later if tests indicate a different drug would be more effective. Many of these infections are resistant to penicillin and other first-line antibiotics, so more expensive second-line antibiotics are used.

Sputum, urine, or blood samples are tested for drug susceptibility to determine whether a bacterial disease is gram-negative.

Malaria

People with chills, headache, fatigue, muscle aches, and other malaria symptoms who have recently traveled to a high-risk area should see their doctor immediately. Malaria tests are not done routinely in the United States, and diagnosis is based on risk factors and symptoms.

The most accurate and widely used lab test for diagnosing malaria has been around for more than one hundred years—examining a drop of blood under a microscope to look for parasites. One such test, called the peripheral smear study for malarial parasites (MP) uses blood from a finger, ear lobe, or arm vein that is smeared on a slide and stained. Red blood cells are then checked to see if they contain malarial parasites. One negative blood smear generally means malaria is not present, but if any suspicion remains, smears are repeated every six to twelve hours for forty-eight hours.

Several tests are done to check drug resistance. In one, malaria patients are given an antimalarial drug and then monitored to see if the parasites clear. Another test obtains blood samples from malaria patients and exposes the samples to different concentrations of antimalarial drugs in a lab. A third type of test looks for genetic markers or mutations in the blood that cause resistance to certain drugs. Genetic markers have been identified for resistance to chloroquine, sulfacoxine-pyrimethamine, and atovaquone. Tests for such markers include polymerase chain reaction and gene sequencing.[16]

Treatment for malaria depends on the severity of the disease, the species of *Plasmodium* parasite, the age and overall health of the patient, and how susceptible the parasites in a certain area are to the drugs. In all cases, treatment should begin within twenty-four hours of the first symptoms; otherwise, the patient could die.

Mild cases can be treated with oral medication; severe cases need IV drugs. Chloroquine is the drug of choice, but parasites are becoming resistant to this drug. If a patient does not improve on chloroquine, other drugs are used, such as quinine, doxycycline, tetracycline, clindamycin, or atovaquone proguanil. Two new malaria treatments, called artemisinin-based combination therapies, are highly effective. However, these drugs are still too expensive for widespread use. The Bill and Melinda Gates Foundation is funding research on a less-expensive synthetic version of this drug.

HIV/AIDS

Blood tests are used to detect HIV and to check on the health of an infected person. The enzyme immunoassay test is done first, using a specimen of blood or saliva. This test is not 100 percent accurate, so a Western blot test or a test called immunofluorescence assay is done to verify the results. Both of these tests measure the amount of HIV antibodies—protein molecules produced by white blood cells that attack and destroy HIV.

Once HIV has been diagnosed, cells in the immune system, called CD4 cells and T-helper cells, are measured with another blood test. These cells are the ones destroyed by HIV. If the cell counts (number of cells) are low, a person's immune system may need bolstering with higher dosages of drugs or different drugs. Viral load tests measure the amount of virus in the blood and are also used to assess how well a person is doing.

Today, people infected with HIV are living many more years by taking drugs that slow down the virus's replication in the body and keep it from developing into AIDS. People take the drugs every day for the rest of their lives. Taking several drugs at once (combination therapy) keeps symptoms at bay and helps postpone drug resistance, which is more apt to occur when a single drug is taken for a long time. Meanwhile, replacement drugs are being developed.

Five types of antiviral drugs are currently on the market, and each works in a different way to ward off AIDS. Two new types of drugs are fusion inhibitors and integrase inhibitors. Fusion inhibitors keep HIV from getting into healthy cells of the immune system and infecting them. Integrase inhibitors cripple integrase, an enzyme HIV needs to get into cells.

Viral load tests and CD4 and T-helper cell counts are not treatments, but they are used to monitor how well drug treatments are working. Blood tests are done every three to six months to check these counts. Drug therapy is successful if the viral load is at levels that are untraceable.

People with HIV also need to take drugs to prevent opportunistic infections—serious illnesses to which they are more susceptible. Tuberculosis is one of these illnesses. Two others are a type of pneumonia called *Pneumocystis jiroveci* and genital herpes. Different drugs are used to treat each opportunistic infection.

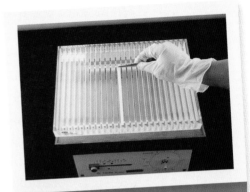

HIV antibodies bind to the nitrocelloluse sheet in a Western blot test, allowing lab technicians to determine whether a person has HIV.

Influenza

Doctors generally diagnose the flu based on symptoms, such as fever, nonproductive cough, and chills. They expect to see many cases during flu season, which lasts from October to May, so they also make their diagnoses based on whether the flu is prevalent at a certain time. They rarely order laboratory tests unless a patient has the flu at an unusual time, has unusual symptoms, or has a serious illness that could turn the flu into a life-threatening disease. Testing is also recommended when a flulike illness occurs in a summer camp, hospital, cruise ship, or other closed setting, to make sure large numbers of people in close contact are treated promptly and appropriately.

Some laboratory tests include viral cultures, polymerase chain reaction tests, and rapid diagnostic tests that give results in only fifteen minutes. However, not all these rapid tests can distinguish between influenza viruses. Specimens are generally taken from the patient's nose. One major advantage of lab tests is that they keep doctors from mistaking the flu for a bacterial infection and prescribing antibiotics unnecessarily.

Treatment for the flu consists of the antiviral drugs Tamiflu and Relenza. They make infections shorter and less severe, but must be taken within forty-eight hours after flu symptoms appear. Some patients with the H1N1 virus had begun developing resistance to these antiviral drugs by the summer of 2009, although it is unclear if a drug-resistant strain had developed and was being transmitted.[17] Flu viruses can develop drug resistance in a number of ways, such as by spontaneously mutating in a single patient treated with an antiviral drug, or by recombining with another variety of flu virus and spreading. In the case of a pandemic flu, when the virus spontaneously mutates in a patient under antiviral treatment, it is not considered a serious public health problem. When a new strain of virus with antiviral resistance begins to circulate in the general population, public health officials face more difficult issues as treatment options narrow for a larger proportion of those infected.

CHAPTER SIX

Outlook for the Future

M icrobes have gotten a bad rap. Actually, most microbes are beneficial and do not cause disease. In a typical human body, bacterial cells outnumber human cells. They are the oldest life form on earth, they outnumber all other species, they generate at least half the oxygen we breathe, and less than one-half of one percent of the estimated two to three billion microbial species have been identified.[1]

We still have a lot to learn about microbes. The U.S. Department of Energy calls them "the roots of life's family tree," because they existed 3.6 billion years ago, long before any other life-form.[2] Studying the genetic makeup of microbes will help scientists understand how these tiny organisms interact with the human body to cause disease and how their genes mutate, pass on these new traits to other microbes, and eventually cause drug-resistant superbugs.

ADVANCES IN TB RESEARCH

TB has been studied for more than one hundred years, but there is still a lot that scientists do not know about the TB bacterium. For example, TB grows very slowly. An old proverb claims "Timing is everything," and that is certainly true for *M. tuberculosis*. Most microbes divide quickly, as often as every fifteen minutes, but *M. tuberculosis* takes a full day to complete one round of cell division and up to two weeks to grow visible quantities in the lab. Robert Koch struggled with the problem of the bacteria's slow growth in the 1880s, and TB researchers are still coping with it today.

Active TB disease can also take a long time to develop once a person is infected. Researchers are still trying to figure out how and why the disease often remains latent for years, and also why many people with latent TB never get active TB at all. Studying how TB bacteria interact with the immune systems of these people is helping scientists develop ways to prevent active disease in other people.

Most microbes divide quickly, as often as every fifteen minutes, but *M. tuberculosis* takes a full day to complete one round of cell division and up to two weeks to grow visible quantities in the lab.

Some light was thrown on these subjects when the *M. tuberculosis* genome was decoded in 1998 as part of the international Human Genome Project. In 2000, scientists worked out the complete sequence of the human genome. This research was a step in understanding how the immune system mounts an attack against TB and other bad bugs, how the TB bacterium protects itself from attack, and why some people can fight the bug off and others cannot. The more scientists understand about genes, the closer they get to developing a new set of drugs that can prevent and cure diseases such as TB.

The TB Cell Wall

The secrets of TB's virulence and its development of drug resistance lie inside its cell walls. Robert Koch, who discovered *M. tuberculosis*, described its unique cell wall in 1882: "It seems likely that the tubercle bacillus is surrounded with a special wall of unusual properties."[3]

Genetics 101

In 1665, Robert Hooke, a German physicist, coined the word *cell* when he looked at a piece of cork under a microscope and saw structures that reminded him of prison cells. Today, we know that cells are the basic structural and functional unit of all living things. Over the years, scientists have investigated cells and made a number of fascinating discoveries. For example, some animals are composed of only one cell, and others, like humans, have 50 trillion cells in their bodies.[4]

Almost every plant, bacteria, and fungi cell has a cell wall, which protects the cell, and a nucleus, a kind of control center that contains genetic (hereditary) information and controls the cell's growth and reproduction. This genetic information is organized in long, threadlike molecules made of deoxyribonucleic acid (DNA), which combine with proteins to form chromosomes. The genes within the chromosomes make up the genome, which contains all of the cell's genetic information.

Humans, animals, plants, and even one-celled bacteria have genomes. Genes make humans who they are, from their eye and hair color to their chance of getting a certain hereditary disease. The genes of bacteria are also blueprints for heredity, determining the characteristics of the cell. The genes tell the bacteria how to multiply, what to infect, and how to make themselves more deadly. The investigation of genes is called genomics.

Robert Hooke's 1665 drawing of cork cells

Scientists can change or manipulate the genetic material in a cell in a process called recombination, or genetic engineering. They do this to try to get cells to perform desired functions. For example, bacteria have been used to produce synthetic insulin, a drug to treat diabetes, since 1982. Scientists took *Escherichia coli* bacteria, a simple, common bacteria, and removed its DNA. Then they took

Continued on next page

Continued from previous page

DNA from the body's insulin-producing cells in the pancreas and put it in the empty nucleus of the *E. coli*. This created *E. coli* bacteria cells programmed to produce insulin instead of the protein they originally produced. This enabled the altered cell to reproduce and create more insulin-producing cells that could be harvested to make human insulin. The discovery revolutionized the production of insulin, which formerly had to be harvested from the pancreases of pigs and cows, because *E. coli* can be cultured in mass quantities, creating lots of human insulin very inexpensively.

This technique has also been used to create human growth hormone and other human and animal hormones. In the future, it may be used to fight TB by making stronger versions of the macrophages, or white blood cells, which kill TB bacteria. Genetic engineering may also be used to improve the BCG vaccine or create new drugs or vaccines for other infectious diseases.

All bacteria have chicken-wire shaped molecules that make their walls rigid and enclose the cell's inner workings. However, *M. tuberculosis* has three more protective layers that shield it from attack. One of the layers contains stringy molecules called mycolic acids that are extremely long and tangled. These molecules produce a cell wall that makes the cell almost waterproof, as if it were waxy. This unusually tight cell wall structure helps explain how the bacterium is able to survive in the lungs for such a long time.

In 1990, Dr. Patrick Brennan of Colorado State University and a team of researchers did some basic research to determine how drugs worked against the TB cell wall. They looked at how the TB cell built the cell wall; perhaps a drug could disrupt that process. First, Brennan and his team genetically manipulated a strain of TB to produce a large amount of the two enzymes that make mycolic acid. Then they tested a new drug, called thiolactomycin (TLM), against both regular TB bacteria and the ones with super-strong mycolic acid-producing enzymes. They found that TLM killed the regular TB cells but not the others.

Basic, Applied, and Clinical Research: Which Is Which?

Basic research, like all research, depends on the scientific method. Scientists make observations about the world, then ask questions such as Why? or How? Then they come up with an explanation—a hypothesis—that they think will answer the question. Next, they design and conduct experiments to test their hypothesis. If the experiments confirm that their explanation is accurate, and results are repeatable, they publish their theory so that other researchers can challenge or reconfirm that the theory is a workable explanation of the world. When experiments contradict a theory, scientists modify their hypothesis. In this way the scientific method produces more and more accurate descriptions of the world and how it works.

Basic research concerns how the world works on very fundamental levels. Scientists seeking to understand how the *M. tuberculosis* microbe lives and reproduces are doing basic research. They seek to find out exactly how this bacterium infects cells, how its construction makes it different from other microbes, and how its biological processes work.

There are two other kinds of research. Applied research builds on basic research by using laboratory animals such as mice to test certain theories about how infections happen or are cured. Animals are often infected or particular breeds are developed with certain conditions so scientists can study them. For example, ob/ob is a strain of mice that was bred to be obese so scientists can study the problems of obesity. Scientists come up with hypotheses about how obesity occurs or can be treated and test their theories on the mice.

Clinical research is conducted on human subjects who are recruited to test certain products or drugs. People who participate in clinical research are fully informed about the nature of the test. In the United States, the Food and Drug Administration regulates this type of research, and it must meet high scientific and ethical standards. The tests, called clinical trials, start out with a very small group of people and then progress to large groups, but only if the drug appears safe and the FDA approves. Approval for a new drug or product can take several years.

The researchers found that TLM works by disrupting one or both of the enzymes and inhibits mycolic acid formation.[5] TLM could overcome the mycolic acid production of regular cells, but not the extra production in the genetically engineered cells. Two of the main TB drugs, INH and ethambutol, also inhibit the creation of mycolic acid, but all three of these drugs work only against TB cells that are dividing and reproducing in the early, more active stage of the disease, not against TB cells that are in the later, latent stage.

Could drugs be developed to destroy TB's cell wall or prevent it from being built in the first place? If so, the bacteria in the active phase would be wide open to destruction by the body's immune system. More research needs to be done on this exciting concept.

In 2001, St. Jude's Children's Research Hospital and the drug company GlaxoSmithKline began developing TLM. They had high hopes that TLM could be used against TB, malaria, staph, and other infections. Although this research further clarified Brennan's findings, it failed to produce an effective new TB drug. Researchers are now trying to modify the structure of TLM to make it a more potent weapon against TB.

Researchers at St. Jude's Children's Research Hospital hope to put many diseases permanently in the past, including TB.

What Is Virulence?

Virulence is the ability of any bacterium, virus, or other infectious microbe to cause disease. It also describes the severity of the disease. The word *virulence* comes from the Latin *virulentia*, meaning a slimy, foul, poisonous liquid—an apt description. A virulent disease is usually infectious, taking a rapid, severe, and deadly course. Without treatment, most of the diseases described in this book are virulent. Some are virulent even after treatment, because the superbugs that cause them are able to fight off the drugs used to treat them.

TB VS. THE IMMUNE SYSTEM

Other areas of ongoing research involve the mystery of how TB continues to live in the body in its latent phase and how it takes in nourishment.

TB grows slowly, but in its early phase of infection, the TB cells do divide and grow actively, faster than they do relative to their growth in later, latent phases. Some researchers study how this pattern of early/active and slow/latent infection protects the TB bacteria from the immune system—and explore how it works, hoping to give doctors and drug developers clues about how to defeat the bacteria.

John McKinney, head of the McKinney Lab at the École Polytechnique Fédérale in Lausanne, Switzerland, and David Russell of Cornell University are among the researchers from several universities who have studied this question. In 2000, Russell's team found that when *M. tuberculosis* goes into the latent state, an enzyme called isocitrate lysase (ICL) keeps it alive by letting the bacteria eat fatty acids, rather than carbohydrates, which are what they eat in the early, active stage of growth.[6] So the team created a mutant strain of

Researcher David Russell contributed to studies that found that without the enzyme isocitrate lysase (ICL), latent TB could be destroyed by the immune system.

M. tuberculosis that could not produce ICL and infected mice with it. They discovered that without ICL, the immune system was able to kill some of the TB bacteria, but not eliminate them.[7]

In 2005, John McKinney's team found that there are two forms of ICL, and when both were deleted from the TB genome, the immune system could completely wipe out the TB bacteria.[8] The findings, published in 2000, launched a drug discovery program. If scientists could inhibit ICL, they would have a major attack weapon against latent TB. Despite additional research, however, scientists have not discovered how to inhibit ICL with drugs.

Researchers are continuing to investigate the relationship between the immune system and latent TB. A 2009 study at Memorial Sloan-Kettering Cancer Center identified a protein called CarD that *M. tuberculosis* needs to survive and help it resist immune attack. When CarD was removed from the bacteria, the bacteria died. Experiments with TB-infected mice showed that TB bacteria depended on CarD in both early and late phases of TB growth. These findings could lead to new drugs to combat TB and other disease-causing microbes.[9]

NEW DRUGS AND DIAGNOSTIC TOOLS

New vaccines, drug treatments, and diagnostic tools being developed to combat TB could have a major impact on the disease once they become available, according to a study by the Vaccine and Infectious Disease Institute at Fred Hutchinson Cancer Research Center. Using a mathematical model, researchers projected that, by 2050, the worldwide incidence of TB could be reduced by 10 to 71 percent. The study came to the following conclusions:

- A new vaccination now being developed for newborns could reduce TB incidence by 39 to 52 percent by 2050.

- New drug regimens being tested that shorten treatment time and combat drug-resistant strains could reduce TB incidence by 10 to 27 percent by 2050.
- New diagnostic tests being developed could decrease TB incidence by 13 to 42 percent by 2050 by getting people to treatment more quickly.
- A combination of vaccinations, drugs, and diagnostic tests would be much more effective, preventing 55.3 million cases of TB and lowering TB incidence by up to 71 percent by 2050.[10]

Scientists are working hard to achieve these goals. The sections that follow describe some of the tools being developed to fight TB.

Better TB Vaccines

Vaccines have not yet been able to conquer TB. The BCG vaccine is still the only vaccine available, and it has been in use since the 1920s. Unfortunately, it provides no protection against pulmonary TB, although it has been estimated to be 80 percent effective against disseminated TB in young children, which affects many areas of the body. For this reason, it is given to 100 million newborns every year, to protect against deadly diseases like TB meningitis.[11]

Why is the BCG vaccine no longer effective against pulmonary TB? Some experts believe that over the years, the production process had weakened the live bacteria too much, until it was a pale imitation of the original.

Researchers at Vanderbilt University Medical Center recently refuted this idea. Their studies show that both the TB bacteria and the BCG vaccine produce substances called antioxidants that help the bacteria dodge the immune system. When they removed the vaccine's ability to produce antioxidants, then gave the altered vaccine to mice infected with TB, it induced a stronger immune response. The study proved that the BCG vaccine had not gotten weaker; it had actually started

What Is a Clinical Trial?

Clinical trials check the effectiveness and safety of new medicines or medical devices by testing them on large groups of people. The federal government, large medical centers, or drug companies often conduct these studies. People with incurable or hard-to-treat diseases often take part in trials because they get a chance to try promising new treatments.

Subjects are usually divided into two groups: a group taking the new drug and a control group taking a

placebo (pronounced "pluh-SEE-boh"), an inactive substance that contains no medication. People do not know whether they get the real drug or the placebo. Other trials test groups of people using a new drug against groups of people using older drugs as well as people receiving a placebo. This lets researchers see how effective a new drug is compared to an older medication or no drug at all. Sometimes, the group taking the placebo also gets better just from the power of suggestion.

People who take part in a clinical trial are usually divided into two groups: those taking a new drug and those taking a placebo, or substance that contains no medication.

doing the opposite of what it was supposed to do because antioxidants were causing it to stifle the immune response.

In 2006, the Aeras Global TB Vaccine Foundation licensed the modification technology developed by the Vanderbilt researchers. The foundation is using this technology and findings from other studies to revamp the BCG vaccine and make it better than ever.[12] This research effort is one of many being conducted to find new TB vaccines or to improve the existing BCG vaccine.

Future plans for the BCG vaccine include using it in a technique called prime boosting. A person would get a prime, or initial, vaccine—either the existing BCG or a new, improved one. Then a booster shot would follow later. Different boosters would be given to different groups of people. For instance, infants and young children with no prior exposure to TB might get one type of preventive booster vaccine, and young adults might get another type. A third type of vaccine might be given to people who have TB, as a treatment along with TB drugs.

A prime-boost strategy should improve protection against TB and also protect people for a longer time. A prime-boost strategy using a new TB vaccine to boost the current BCG vaccine is thought to be the best way to introduce a new vaccine into countries with high rates of TB.

Researchers are using a variety of techniques to develop new types of TB vaccines. One important

During gene splicing, a recombinant virus will splice its genes (orange) into a cell's DNA (blue).

technique is gene splicing, which creates recombinant (genetically engineered) vaccines. A new type of BCG vaccine is being developed this way, by cutting apart DNA from TB bacteria and attaching it to bacteria in the BCG vaccine. When this new vaccine enters the body, it stimulates the immune system to produce antibodies against TB. Some of the antibodies match up with TB proteins, and others match up with BCG proteins. If someone is infected with TB, the body has a pattern on file for producing antibodies to fight off TB germs. This new vaccine will contain only a small number of TB genes, not whole live disease germs.

Fifty TB vaccines are currently being tested around the world, but only two are expected to enter the last step in the testing process by 2011. It can take fifteen years—from discovery to getting a license—for a vaccine to reach developing countries, according to the WHO.[13]

New TB Drugs

Research into new drugs for TB is advancing on many fronts—and not a moment too soon. The last TB drug approved by the FDA was rifampicin, back in 1971. The consensus among scientists is that new drug regimens must be shorter and use fewer drugs, so people will be more likely to comply. Several new drugs are in various stages of development now.

Sometimes, using existing drugs in a new way can be as good as finding new drugs.

In June 2007, human clinical trials started for a promising new antibiotic called PA-824. The new drug appears to attack TB bacteria in both the dividing and slow-growing stages, perhaps reducing the time needed to cure the disease in humans. It also may target MDR-TB. In animal studies, the drug was found to have bacterial killing effects similar to the first-line TB drugs isoniazid and rifampin. Especially promising is the fact that PA-824 does not interact with certain liver enzymes, which makes if safer for people co-infected with HIV. Current TB drugs often cause serious adverse effects when used with drugs to treat HIV.

Several other drugs are also being tested. One, called TMC207, shows promise in people with drug-resistant TB. In a study of forty-seven TB patients with MDR-TB, half were given TMC207 along with other standard TB drugs and half were given standard TB drugs plus a placebo. Of the patients receiving TMC207, almost half had negative sputum cultures after eight weeks on the drug—better than on standard TB drugs alone.[14]

Sometimes, using existing drugs in a new way can be as good as finding new drugs. In 2009, researchers at the University of California, San Diego, found that entacapone and tolcapone, drugs for Parkinson's disease (a brain disorder), might be effective against MDR-TB and XDR-TB. Using computers and lab experiments, they learned that these drugs inhibit *M. tuberculosis* without harming the body's cells. "Repurposing" existing drugs has obvious advantages, including the fact that the drugs have already gone through the long FDA approval process.[15]

Another way to use an existing drug is known as the "kitchen sink approach." A scientist takes an old drug and develops thousands of compounds from it that differ only slightly. Researchers used ethambutol, an established TB drug, and created more than 100,000 variations of it. Then they took seventy of the most potent compounds, narrowed them down to six, and tested them on mice. They found one candidate, SQ-109, that races to the lungs and kills TB bacteria instead of just halting their growth as some other TB drugs do. In mice, SQ-109 proved to be highly effective against MDR-TB, especially when combined with rifampin. The drug still must be carefully tested on humans, however.[16]

Improved Diagnostic Tests

The spread of MDR-TB—which is more difficult to treat and thus more lethal—is likely to accelerate until there are quick, simple, inexpensive tests for antibiotic susceptibility that can be used anywhere in the world. Without good screening methods for MDR-TB, clinics and hospitals cannot effectively quarantine TB patients with drug-resistant strains. While waiting for test results, doctors are also reduced to a trial-and-error method of prescribing medicine, and very sick TB patients do not have time for false starts. The tests that follow are some that are being developed or have recently become available.

Xpert MTB/RIF: This test uses a sputum sample to tell if a person has MDR-TB that is resistant to rifampicin or TB that can be treated with common drugs. Results are available in only two hours, and the entire process takes place in a sealed plastic cartridge that cannot be contaminated, which could cause false results. This test is ideal for countries with limited resources because it does not require expensive equipment to extract *M. tuberculosis* DNA from sputum. Instead, sputum is liquefied by adding chemicals to the collection cup and is then transferred into the cartridge to be processed. The test became available in 2009.[17]

Rats Sniff Out TB in Africa

In South Africa, rats are being used to sniff out *M. tuberculosis* in laboratory samples. These are not just any rats, but raccoon-sized African giant pouched rats dubbed "Hero Rats." Their ultra-sharp sense of smell allows them to quickly detect TB bacteria in sputum samples.

Hero Rats are trained to signal with paw motions when they sniff a sputum sample containing TB bacteria. As a reward, they receive a nut or a piece of fruit. Each rat can evaluate one hundred sputum samples in about twenty minutes. Forty samples in twenty-four hours is the WHO's standard for a technician using a microscope. Besides being faster, rats are also cheaper, more reliable detectors than the usual lab test, which is called sputum smear microscopy. They can also detect TB bacteria in samples that human evaluators previously thought were negative. This suggests that the rodents may be able to nose out TB at a very early stage of the disease.

South Africa has the highest incidence of TB in the world (948 infections for every 100,000 people). Forty-four percent of all TB patients are also co-infected with HIV/AIDS. Early detection is a critical step in stopping the epidemic, and widespread use of the rats could be an important part of this process.[18]

Hero Rats can detect TB much more quickly and accurately than standard lab tests.

TB Breathalyser: This test is much quicker and more accurate than the Mantoux test. Patients cough into a collection tube; the bottom of the tube is coated with a chemical that reacts to TB bacteria. The tube is then sealed and inserted into a reader to get results in just a few minutes. The test is easy to use, even by people who have little or no medical training, and does not require sterile conditions, so it is well-suited for developing countries.[19]

Transdermal patch: The patch is applied to the skin like an adhesive bandage and diagnoses active TB infection. (The Mantoux test cannot distinguish between active and latent infection.) The patch delivers a protein into the skin that is found in TB bacteria. If a person has active TB, the skin under the patch will become red and may form a blister. Results take three to four days (slightly longer than the Mantoux test). Unlike the Mantoux test, this test will not give false positive results in people vaccinated with BCG, infected with other mycobacteria, or just finishing TB treatment.[20]

Line-probe assay: The line-probe assay test uses a technique called polymerase chain reaction (PCR) to analyze the DNA of TB cells. PCR is the same method that investigators use to analyze the DNA left at crime scenes. Researchers have developed ways to use PCR so that when applied to TB cells it can identify not only regular TB but also TB that is rifampin-resistant.[21]

WHAT'S AHEAD FOR OTHER SUPERBUGS?

Faster, more accurate diagnostic tests, improved vaccines, and new drugs to replace those that have become less effective are the keys to fighting off superbugs in the future. Since 1998, about a dozen new antimicrobial drugs have become available, but the microbes are already becoming resistant to many of them. Several more drugs are in development, awaiting FDA approval. Because of this, the following sections concentrate on promising research, new diagnostic tests, and innovative equipment that is already on the market or close to being available.

Smart New Use for Old Technology

Technological developments that revolutionize the way people solve problems can arise from unexpected places. One example is how TB researchers borrowed technology from the Beagle 2, the landing craft lost during the European Space Agency's Mars Express mission in 2003.

The Beagle 2 was equipped with a compact unit that used gas chromatography/mass spectrometry (GC-MS) to analyze matter. Scientists hoped this unit would help determine if any type of life existed on Mars. Unfortunately, the probe disappeared in the Martian atmosphere. Four years later, the unit's maker, British scientist Colin Pillinger, convinced the leaders of the space program to turn the GC-MS technology into a clinical tool for detecting TB.

A simulated image of the Beagle 2 on Mars

GC-MS breaks apart a sample into ions (charged particles) and measures their mass. This information can be used to identify substances. Pillinger and a colleague, Geraint Morgan, took the GC-MS technology and created a microwave-oven-sized device that searches for particles on the waxy coat of the cell wall of *M. tuberculosis*. The device is easy to use, it quickly and accurately detects TB, and it is small enough to travel anywhere in the world. In the poorest countries, where diagnostic tools and trained health-care workers are lacking, this portable detection unit could make a big difference.

MRSA

Every year, MRSA infects about 94,000 people and kills 19,000 of them.[22] But the bacterium that causes MRSA, *S. aureus*, does not make everyone sick. About one-third of all people have staph on their skin or in their noses. They can pass the germ on to others through a wound, catheter site, or IV site without even realizing they are infected.

Why do some people get sick and not others? Researchers are trying to find out. Solving this puzzle will help them develop new ways to prevent and treat staph infections and perhaps prevent MRSA from ever occurring.

A step in the right direction occurred in 2009, when a team of Canadian researchers discovered an interesting aspect of MRSA. In some people, the immune system senses MRSA and overreacts, leading to severe inflammation and sometimes even toxic shock, which shuts down vital organ systems and can lead to death. However, the MRSA bacteria's cell walls contain special molecules that bind to immune system cell walls. This encourages the production of IL-10, a type of protein that helps to keep the immune system from overreacting.

Why does the immune system get out of control in some people? No one knows. But understanding how MRSA works with the immune system may help researchers develop drugs that can bind tightly to immune cells and stimulate production of IL-10. But such drugs are still years away.[23]

In the meantime, new diagnostic tests for MRSA look promising. These tests may soon grow into a billion-dollar business for drug companies, market analysts say. The tests do not require culturing in a lab or specially trained workers and can generate results in only a few hours. This is a huge improvement over the usual forty-eight hours. The faster people are diagnosed, the faster they can start treatment. This increases their chance of making a full recovery and decreases their chance of infecting others.

Xpert MRSA is a diagnostic test that can determine whether a person has MRSA in as few as two hours.

One such test is the Xpert MRSA. Results are available in only two hours, so doctors can begin MRSA treatment quickly. Tissue samples are placed in a cartridge and loaded into a molecular diagnostic device, which then analyzes the sample.[24]

Another test uses bacteriophages—viruses that infect bacteria—to identify staph and determine what drugs it is sensitive to. A sample of blood is combined with a mixture containing the bacteriophages and a growth medium and kept at 35°C for five hours. Afterward, a few drops of the mixture are put on a detector strip. If bars appear on the strip, MRSA is present.[25]

Streptococcus Pneumoniae Disease

The NOW Streptococcus Test is an easy-to-use, rapid test that identifies *S. pneumoniae* within fifteen minutes. The test identifies the *S. pneumoniae* antigen in the urine of patients with pneumonia and in the cerebrospinal fluid of patients with meningitis. It is meant to be used along with cultures and X-rays to diagnose pneumococcal pneumonia and meningitis.[26]

Gram-Negative Bacterial Diseases

One of the surest ways to prevent gram-negative bacterial diseases in hospitals is by improved infection control measures. These range from simple hand washing to new devices and technologies to control the spread of infection. Researchers are working on several techniques that show potential.

One new idea is coating medical devices like catheters and surgical instruments with penicillin. The technique was developed by researchers at the University of Southern Mississippi, who found a way to modify the surfaces of devices so penicillin would stick to them. Experiments showed that the antibiotic-coated surfaces killed staph. The team hopes to find other antibiotics that will adhere to surfaces and kill bacteria that are resistant to penicillin.[27]

Chlorine-coated bed linens are a new technology that repels microbes, even after sheets and pillowcases are repeatedly laundered. These linens are already available. A hand sanitizer for gloved hands is in the planning stages. It sterilizes hands in three seconds using Ultraviolet C emitted through a germicidal tube, so potentially harmful chemicals are not needed.

Research is also being done on copper versus stainless steel surfaces in hospitals. In a 2008 study at the Selly Oak Hospital in England, a set of sink fixtures, a push plate on a door, and a toilet seat were replaced with copper versions. They were swabbed twice a day for ten weeks for germs and compared to swabs from a traditional sink fixture, push plate, and toilet seat. The copper items had up to 95 percent fewer MRSA, influenza, and other microbes on their surfaces. The healing power of copper is nothing new. Copper was used by the ancient Egyptians to sterilize leg wounds and drinking water, and Hippocrates used it to treat leg ulcers. Many of today's medicines contain copper. Copper may become the next big bacteria-fighting tool in hospitals.[28]

One of the surest ways to prevent gram-negative bacterial diseases in hospitals is by improved infection control measures.

Malaria

Every year, 350 to 500 million people around the world (mostly in sub-Saharan Africa) are diagnosed with malaria, and about one million die.[29] Most people die from lack of treatment, but some die because the treatments no longer work. For years, chloroquine was the drug of choice to kill *P. falciparum*, a one-celled parasite carried by mosquitoes that can cause malaria.

But resistance to this drug is spreading, along with resistance to another commonly used drug, sulfacoxine-pyrimethamine.

Researchers at the Johns Hopkins Bloomberg School of Public Health are tackling the problem by genetically modifying mosquitoes. By "switching off" two genes so that they were no longer expressed in the mosquitoes' genetic codes, they were able to block the development of the malaria-causing parasite in the gut tissue of mosquitoes. They did this by activating the insect's immune response before it became infected by the parasite, so it could fight it off. In the wild, this response is believed to occur too late to prevent the parasite from breeding in the mosquitoes. The researchers hope that before long, these techniques can be used to make the mosquitoes incapable of transmitting the malaria parasite. Gene research is also being used to decrease the number of mosquitoes worldwide.[30]

A new malaria vaccine is also in the planning stages. Human testing is scheduled to start in early 2010 at Walter Reed Army Medical Center. The vaccine has protected mice 100 percent against malaria, and researchers are aiming for at least 90 percent protection in humans. The Bill and Melinda Gates Foundation is funding the $17-million project. Even if human testing goes well, it may be ten years before the vaccine is approved by the FDA.[31]

HIV/AIDS

By 2009, nearly two hundred human clinical trials had been conducted to find a vaccine to prevent HIV infection.[32] There are also many new drugs being developed, including those to use when drug resistance occurs. In addition, gene therapies are being investigated. For example, several types of gene therapy approaches are being studied to see if T cells can be made to resist HIV infection. There are currently several lab tests to determine drug resistance. These tests are expensive and results can take over one month, but cheaper, faster tests are being developed.

HOW REAL PEOPLE DEAL: BITTEN BY THE BUG—TWICE

Andrew Wylde, a twenty-four-year-old investment banker from London, was doing volunteer work in Ghana, Africa, teaching in a rural school. Every night at 6 P.M., he and his fellow volunteers played soccer, about the time the mosquitoes came out. One night they stayed out a little later than usual, and Andrew got a lot of bites. But he had been pretty faithful about taking his antimalarial medicine, so he did not give it much thought.

Three or four days later, Andrew became extremely ill with diarrhea, aches, and sweats. At first, he told himself it was the heat or something he ate, but then it suddenly hit him hard. "I just started to sweat so hard my head began pounding," he said. He went to the hospital and they diagnosed him quickly with malaria. "It was in the latter stages," Andrew said. Later, the doctor told him he had been just twelve hours away from dying.

Andrew was hooked up to IVs to pump him full of drugs and replace the fluids he had lost. He was so sick, he did not leave his bed for two weeks. He also lost an alarming amount of weight. He kept the news from his parents for a couple weeks, and when he finally told them, he said "they freaked out."

Andrew was stunned when only a month later, he got malaria again. He does not even remember getting bitten. This time, he went straight to the doctor and it only took him a week to recover. That is when he noticed the difference between how the Westerners and the locals were treated when they got sick.

Even though Andrew Wylde took his malaria pills, he still contracted the disease during a volunteer trip to Ghana in 2009.

"I knew a couple of the kids in the school I was working in who died from malaria, and that was such a tragic experience," Andrew said. "I was lucky enough to have a hospital very close to where I was staying, but it can take about twenty hours to get to somewhere suitable in some of the rural areas when people are traveling on foot. The second time I got malaria, I went to one of the best doctors in the region. I even went to his house, where there were pictures of him shaking hands with the pope and Bill Clinton. I doubt most (local) people would have had that opportunity."

Andrew blames catching malaria on not taking his anti-malarial drug as regularly as he should have. "It won't stop me traveling," he said. "When it comes to malaria, chances are you're going to be bitten by something. Even then, you should be wary about assuming tablets are a vaccine rather than a preventive measure. If you get bitten by ten mosquitoes in a night and one of them has malaria, the drug will probably do its job. But if you get bitten by forty, and half of them are carrying it, then you might not be so lucky."[33]

Influenza

Japanese scientists have reported a discovery that could lead to a new type of antiviral drug that could combat drug resistance in influenza. Tamiflu and Relenza, the drugs now used to treat flu, stop the virus from reproducing by blocking key proteins. But the viruses can mutate into drug-resistant strains. Using cell cultures, researchers have identified some drugs that might block the first step in the infection process and keep flu viruses from infecting cells in the first place. This research could lead to a new way to design antiviral drugs and drugs for other medical problems.[34]

CHAPTER SEVEN

Living With TB and Other Superbugs

A round the world, more people die of infectious diseases than of any other single cause.[1] That means many, many people are also *living* with infectious diseases. Some of these diseases last a lifetime (like HIV/AIDS), others are curable but often come back (like malaria), and many leave people with permanent disabilities (like MRSA).

The diseases discussed in this book are very different, but they also have a lot in common. For one thing, they are all contagious, which creates a climate of fear and misunderstanding among the public. This is especially true of TB and HIV/AIDS. Another common thread is that all of these diseases are becoming drug resistant. Being diagnosed with an infectious disease is frightening enough. Learning that doctors do not have drugs to treat the disease is terrifying.

How do people live with infectious diseases or their aftermath? How do their families cope? How do they get on with their lives after they are cured?

The road from the first TB symptoms to the final day of treatment is long and hard, no matter who a person is or where he or she lives. But having TB in the United States is different from having TB in developing countries like those in Africa.

TB IN THE UNITED STATES

People who have TB are usually frightened and confused by their symptoms. Coughing and night sweats may be mistaken for a bad case of the flu, and people often buy cough medicine to treat it. When the medicine does not help and they get sicker, lose weight, and feel exhausted, they realize it is more than the flu and go to the doctor.

Because TB is no longer common in the United States, doctors often misdiagnose it. This is especially true if the patient is well-dressed, employed, and otherwise in good health—in other words, not a typical TB patient. Doctors are more apt to consider TB if a patient is a recent immigrant, lives in a homeless shelter, has AIDS, or has any of the other risk factors for TB.

This means that a lot of people get sent home with flu remedies or other treatments that will not cure their TB. By the time they return to the doctor and get tested for TB, they have exposed

fact OR fiction

Only Poor or Homeless People Get TB

Not true. Being poor or homeless are risk factors for TB, but no one is immune to the disease. In Contra Costa County, California, clusters of TB cases were recently found in an affluent high school (twelve cases) and in young, healthy people who frequented the same club (five people). Cases in the county suddenly increased from fifty-one in 2007 to seventy-nine in 2008, and public health officials were concerned. They blamed the sudden increase on latent infections becoming active, and they pointed to the economic recession as a contributing factor. With people losing their homes, two families might be living in a house now instead of one, and crowded conditions create a perfect climate for TB transmission.

"Everybody breathes," said Dr. Charles Crane, medical director of the Contra Costa Health Services' TB program. "It isn't just a disease for immigrants, it is a threat to everybody."[2]

Tuberculosis can strike anyone, including otherwise healthy teenagers.

many more people and the TB bacteria have done even more damage to their bodies. The quicker TB is treated, the better.

Unless someone they know has TB, most people have no idea what TB treatment involves. The testing process alone can be nerve-wracking. A Mantoux test and chest X-ray can reveal if someone has been infected, but they cannot distinguish between latent and active disease or tell if the bacteria are drug resistant. A sputum culture can do this, but TB bacteria grow so slowly, the results can take up to eight weeks. In the meantime, the doctor will prescribe antibiotics and hope they work. If the culture results show the patient has MDR-TB, he will need much stronger drugs and may have lost up to two months of treatment.

The treatment itself is grueling. Patients with active drug-resistant TB must take four drugs daily for six to twelve months, and many of them have unpleasant side effects, such as nausea and vomiting. Some can even cause permanent deafness, vision problems, and a liver disease called hepatitis. Patients with latent TB are more easily treated—they generally need to take only one drug for six to nine months. Patients with drug-resistant TB need treatment for up to two years, and some of them require surgery to remove or repair diseased lung tissue.

On top of this, patients have to be isolated to prevent the spread of TB. When they receive their diagnosis at the doctor's office, many people are given a mask to wear and admitted to the hospital immediately. Once there, they are isolated in a special negative pressure room where air constantly flows in and is filtered when it flows back out. Everyone who enters the room must be gowned and masked, and the patient may not be allowed any visitors. When several sputum tests show patients are no longer contagious, they will be sent home.

All patients who are diagnosed with TB must wear a mask and be isolated from others to prevent spreading the disease.

Patients who are not acutely ill will be placed on home isolation. They are required

What Is Ototoxicity?

Ototoxicity is damage to the inner ear caused by a drug or chemical, resulting in hearing loss. A class of drugs known as aminoglycosides, and one drug called capreomycin—potent antibiotics given for MDR-TB and XDR-TB—can cause permanent hearing loss. Unfortunately, these are among the few drugs that are effective in curing drug-resistant TB. Even after patients stop taking these drugs, they stay in the ear tissue for up to six months.

Hearing loss is a sad outcome for any TB patient, but it is especially sad in developing countries where so many patients have drug-resistant TB. These countries will soon be faced with yet another problem: how to deal with hearing loss in a significant number of their population. A gene mutation is thought to put some people at particular risk of hearing loss, so genetic testing may help identify them before the drugs are given.

by law to stay in their house or yard except to go to the doctor. No one is allowed to visit except a public health worker, who usually comes every day to make sure patients take their medicine. This feels a lot like being under house arrest for committing a crime. Isolation is extremely difficult for patients and makes them feel like social outcasts.

People with TB also worry about exposing their families, friends, and co-workers to the disease. Everyone who has been in close contact is required to get tested for TB. Anyone who tests positive must notify their close contacts. Knowing they might have given other people a serious disease and the snowball effect it creates only makes TB patients feel more guilty and ashamed.

After tests show the person is no longer infectious, he can resume his normal life. But going back to work, school, or social activities can be hard, especially for teenagers. Friends may not be able to relate to what a teen with TB has been through or may think the person is still contagious. Teens who were isolated for weeks or months may not feel well enough to study and then have trouble catching up. Phone calls, text messaging, and emailing can help teens feel less cut off, but isolation with a contagious disease is still very hard.

TB IN AFRICA

People in Africa live with TB every day and know the symptoms. But this does not mean they seek treatment right away. The disease may be prevalent, but that does not make people more tolerant of it. Just the opposite. The thought of being a social outcast may cause people to hide their disease out of fear. If they are sick, they might think no one will want to marry them or worry they will lose their jobs. If they are already married, they may worry they will not be able to support their families while they are in the hospital.

Because of these fears, some people go to village healers who promise quick cures instead of seeing a medical doctor. By the time they realize the herbs or other folk remedies are not working, their TB is in an advanced stage. People also put off getting treatment because hospitals and clinics are often far away and traveling by bus is expensive.

Once they receive medical treatment, the medicine to cure TB is usually free or very inexpensive. However, many people do not finish all their pills because they do not understand the instructions. Others sell their drugs because they need the money. Often people start feeling better and stop taking the drugs. For these people, the DOTS program, where patients are observed taking their drugs every day, can be a lifesaver. But there are not always enough health-care workers to go around, and family members are not always dependable observers.

In Africa, being in isolation for TB can feel like prison. Because so many people have MDR-TB and XDR-TB, patients in South Africa are quarantined in hospitals surrounded by razor wire. Health officials hope this forced isolation will keep

Comic Book Has Serious Message

Luis Figo, an international soccer star from Portugal, stars in a comic book that provides important information on TB prevention and TB's relationship to HIV. *Luis Figo and the World Tuberculosis Cup* features a team of teenagers with the soccer star as the captain. They play soccer against a squad of TB germs and win. The book is available in ten languages, and 70,000 free copies have been distributed in several countries. It was produced by the Stop TB Partnership (a WHO initiative) and UNAIDS.[3]

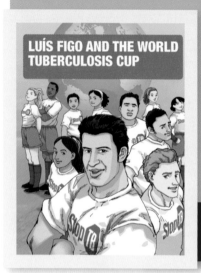

Luis Figo and his team of teenagers play and win against TB germs in *Luis Figo and the World Tuberculosis Cup*.

TB from spreading to the 5 to 7 million people with HIV/AIDS. The law says that all patients with drug-resistant TB must be kept in isolation for six months or until their test results are negative. But many people are being kept longer without their consent, and there have been several mass escapes from these hospitals.

In Africa, being in isolation for TB can feel like prison. Because so many people have MDR-TB and XDR-TB, patients in South Africa are quarantined in hospitals surrounded by razor wire.

A pilot program in South Africa has allowed thirty-seven patients—thirteen with XDR-TB—to be isolated at home and receive treatment.[4] But public health officials are worried about the safety of sending them home, because there is no way to monitor whether they are actually staying at home. The debate about forced isolation is ongoing in South Africa.

LIVING WITH OTHER SUPERBUGS

Living With MRSA

Sometimes, a MRSA infection can be cured with antibiotics and the patient ends up as healthy as before. But a MRSA infection can also kill, disfigure, or permanently disable someone. According to a 2007 study published in the *Journal of Pediatric Critical Care Medicine*, MRSA is more deadly and dangerous when it strikes healthy young people. Doctors are still trying to figure out why.[5]

MRSA is prevalent among athletes of all ages because they get frequent cuts and scrapes and have a lot of body contact, which can spread the bacteria from player to player. What is it like to live with a serious MRSA infection? Former Washington Redskins defensive tackle, Brandon Noble, experienced how it can change a person's life.

HOW REAL PEOPLE DEAL: A FOOTBALL PLAYER TACKLED BY STAPH

A lineman for the Cleveland Browns, Brian Russell was used to getting hit hard during a football game—and then hitting back. But he was no match for *Staphylococcus aureus* (staph), the microscopic germ that tackled him during the 2006 preseason.

"I went from being in tiptop shape, to a few hours later, being knocked on my butt and having surgery," Brian said. "It happened just like that."[6]

It started with a scraped elbow, which seemed like no big deal. Brian was used to aches and pains from getting clobbered by 250-pound running backs. He had just finished

---

Antibiotics cured NFL football player Brian Russell's staph infection, but some strains of staph are becoming resistant to these medications.

training camp in Buffalo, New York, and figured he had scraped his elbow on the artificial turf. But a few days later, he started feeling sick, and his elbow got painful and extremely swollen. So he went to the hospital.

Tests revealed that Brian had a staph infection. Luckily, the doctors diagnosed the infection right away and treated it with antibiotics. Brian recovered, but he now wears long sleeves during practices and games and will never assume a cut is harmless again.

Although Brian went through an ordeal, he was lucky his staph infection was treatable with common antibiotics. Not everyone is so lucky. One strain of the bacteria—methicillin-resistant *S. aureus* (MRSA) has become resistant to most antibiotics and can swiftly overtake the body. Ricky Lannetti, a twenty-one year-old star football player at a Pennsylvania college, died of a MRSA infection in 2004. A wrestler at a California high school, Noah Armendariz, died of complications of a MRSA infection in 2008.

Several professional football and basketball players have also become infected with MRSA in recent years. NBA All-Star Grant Hill got MRSA in his ankle and ran such a high fever that he had convulsions. It took him six months to recover, but he resumed his basketball career.

Teams have stepped up their efforts to control MRSA by disinfecting locker rooms and equipment, cleaning and covering even minor cuts right away, and drilling players on good locker room hygiene. A 2009 report by two infectious disease experts said the rate of MRSA is declining in the NFL. There were sixty infections reported between 2003 and 2005 and only thirty-three between 2006 and 2008. So efforts are beginning to pay off.[7]

In one year, when Brandon was thirty-one years old, he was treated for two severe MRSA infections. In 2005, after minor surgery on his right knee, he expected to be ready to play football that season. But after the stitches were removed, he noticed a quarter-sized red mark on his knee. Soon, he experienced flu-like symptoms and his knee felt like it was on

After getting MRSA twice, former NFL player Brandon Noble takes no chances around his kids, making sure that they always keep their hands clean.

fire. By the time Brandon was readmitted to the hospital two days later, his whole leg was discolored. He was diagnosed with MRSA.

"One of the first doctors that I saw told my parents that if I had waited another twenty-four hours we could be talking about the loss of my leg—or worse," he said.[8]

In the hospital, Brandon was given powerful IV antibiotics. After he went home, he learned how to give himself vancomycin through a catheter in his arm. It took one and a half hours three times a day. He was not allowed to lift anything over five pounds with that arm, which was hard since he had young children.

Brandon was so exhausted that even going to Redskins Park to watch practice and have his knee iced wore him out. He had to take a two– or three-hour nap every afternoon. But he finally felt well enough to start building up the muscles in his bad leg. He returned to training camp that summer, but unfortunately hurt his other knee. After another surgery, he was placed on injured reserve and sat out the season.

While he was recuperating at home, Brandon helped his wife take care of the kids. Chasing them around, he re-injured his left knee. The doctors drained fluid out of it several times over a few weeks. Brandon was devastated when he started developing flulike symptoms and burning pain again. This time, his doctor knew it was MRSA; Brandon had more surgery, and returned home on IV antibiotics again.

MRSA is prevalent among athletes of all ages because they get frequent cuts and scrapes and have a lot of body contact, which can spread the bacteria from player to player.

Although the infection cleared up, Brandon's thigh muscles completely atrophied (wasted away). He also developed blood clots in both legs. On top of all this, the antibiotics killed all the good bacteria in his stomach and intestines that help digest food, so he was only able to eat bagels and yogurt. He lost thirty-five pounds.

Brandon hoped to return to football, but blood clots and MRSA ended his football career. He now coaches at the college level. He worries about his family getting MRSA and gets scared when his kids get a cut or scratch. He keeps antibacterial soaps all over the house, which he sprays on his kids' hands all the time.

The infection cost him his career, affected his health for years, and almost cost him his life. It had a huge impact on his family. "I can't imagine having my children or wife go through it," he said. "That would kill me."[9]

Living With Streptococcal Pneumonia

Sinus infections and ear infections caused by a pneumococcal infection are not usually serious conditions. But in people with weakened immune systems, they can progress to meningitis. This brain infection can kill patients within twenty-four hours of getting symptoms. It can also cause deafness, paralysis, mental retardation, and limb loss. People with these disabilities and their families face countless challenges, but many people learn to cope with the loss of limbs and other disabilities.

There are many online and community-based support groups for people living with meningitis and families of people who have died of this disease.

Living With Gram-Negative Bacterial Disease

People who contract gram-negative bacterial diseases are almost always in the hospital. These diseases most often occur in intensive care units, after surgery, in very old or very young patients, or in burn patients—in other words, in patients who are already very ill or who have weakened immune systems. These infections are caused by many different bacteria, and all are potentially deadly. Patients who survive these infections are often left with permanent disabilities. For example, *Klebsiella pneumoniae* can cause pulmonary gangrene, leading to destruction of part of the lung. Living with a disability is hard on both patients and families.

Living With Malaria

People in countries with a risk of malaria—such as in Central and South America, Africa, and Asia—live with the mosquitoes that can cause malaria every day. Eventually, through repeated exposure, they build up immunity to severe disease. However, young children, pregnant women, people with weakened immune systems, and travelers from other countries have little or no immunity and are at high risk of getting sick and dying if they do not take precautions.

If malaria does not kill people, it can leave them with permanent nerve damage, including lack of coordination, speech problems, and epilepsy, which causes seizures. Other disabilities include severe anemia (lack of red blood cells), pulmonary edema (fluid in the lungs), kidney failure, low blood sugar, and irregular heartbeats. If a pregnant woman gets malaria, she can pass the infection on to her baby. She is also at increased risk of having a miscarriage, a stillbirth, a premature delivery, or a baby with low birth weight.

Even when malaria is cured, the parasite may remain dormant in the liver and cause a relapse months or years later.

This can occur if the disease is treated with the wrong drug or the right drug at the wrong dose for too short a time. It can also occur if the parasite becomes resistant to the drug and renders it ineffective.

If malaria does not kill people, it can leave them with permanent nerve damage, including lack of coordination, speech problems, and epilepsy, which causes seizures.

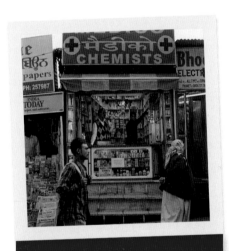

A local pharmacy in Chail, India. American travelers should obtain their anti-malarial drugs in the United States, as drugs sold in countries with a risk of malaria could be ineffective in preventing the disease.

People who live in countries with a risk of malaria are not the only ones who have to worry. Many American students are traveling these days, and foreign students who come to America are returning home to countries where malaria is common. Long before students pack their backpacks—about eight weeks before departure—they need to visit their doctor and start taking antimalarial medicine. They need to continue this medicine during their trip and after they get home. Students returning to their home countries should also take antimalarial drugs because they have lost their natural immunity.

People should buy these drugs in the United States, not in countries with a risk of malaria. Antimalarial drugs in countries with a risk of malaria can be of poor quality, contain contaminants, or be counterfeit and not provide protection against malaria. Students and other travelers also need to pack insect repellant and an insecticide-treated bed net. These measures are 90 to 100 percent effective against malaria.[10]

Living With TB-HIV

Patients say that the social stigma attached to TB is even worse than that of HIV/AIDS. A patient with HIV who then develops TB must endure the lonely ordeal of six weeks of hospital isolation followed by six weeks of home isolation. The TB drugs can cause severe side effects, including fatigue, skin problems, and sleeplessness. They also make the HIV drugs less effective, weakening a dual-diagnosis patient's immune system. Even worse, some patients recover from TB only to get the cold shoulder from the HIV/AIDS community, which had previously been an important source of support, because people in HIV support groups can be very afraid of catching TB.

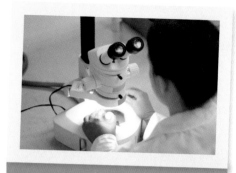

Someday, researchers may discover vaccines for many of today's deadliest diseases, making them a memory of the past.

In developing countries, the problem of getting good care is even harder for people with TB-HIV. Because there is not enough integrated care—that is, programs that combine HIV/AIDS and TB treatment—patients have to go to one clinic for their TB drugs and another clinic for their HIV drugs. In addition, health-care workers in HIV/AIDS clinics often are not up-to-date on treating TB and vice versa. In Africa, where the leading killer of people with HIV is TB, a coordinated effort is a matter of life and death.

The Stop TB Partnership has a goal: to eliminate TB as a public health problem by 2050. That goal seems attainable; polio was thought to be eradicated as a widespread problem in the early 1950s. Yet more and more microbes become drug resistant. Researchers are working against the clock to find new drugs, vaccines, and tests to treat, prevent, and diagnose TB, malaria, MRSA, and other infectious diseases. Perhaps in 2050, people reading this book will tell their grandchildren about the days when superbugs caused deadly diseases, before super *vaccines* came along and wiped them out.

TB and Superbug Timeline

c. 4000 B.C.: Signs of tuberculosis (TB) are preserved in the skeletons of prehistoric man.

c. 3000–2400 B.C.: Signs of TB are preserved in the spines of Egyptian mummies.

2700 B.C.: Malaria is first described in Chinese medical writings.

c. 460 B.C.: Greek physician Hippocrates describes a disease called *phthisis* meaning "to waste away." *Phthisis* is often translated as "consumption" since patients seemed to be consumed by it. Many modern researchers identify this as TB.

c. 1000 A.D.: Persian physician Ibn Sina recognizes TB as a contagious disease.

1679: Dutch physician Franciscus Sylvius describes tubercles in the lungs of those who have died of consumption.

1720: Benjamin Marten, British physician, writes in *A New Theory of Consumptions* (1720) that the disease is spread by long exposure to infected people.

1816: French doctor René-Théophile-Hyacinthe Laënnec invents the stethoscope, allowing physicians to listen to a patient's lungs with greater accuracy.

1839: German medical professor Johann Lukas Schönlein uses the word *tuberculosis* for the first time to describe the disease.

1859: The first sanatorium for the treatment of TB opens in the mountains of Germany.

1863: French biologist Casimir-Joseph Davaine observes microorganisms in the bloodstreams of diseased people.

1880: Charles Louis Alphonse Laveran, a French military surgeon, discovers the parasite that causes malaria.

1882: German scientist Robert Koch finds the tubercle bacillus in infected individuals.

1885: American doctor Edward Trudeau opens the first TB sanatorium in the United States, in Saranac Lake, New York, in the Adirondack Mountains.

1890: Koch announces his creation of a TB vaccine; it later proves ineffective as a vaccine but useful as a diagnostic test.

1905: Koch receives the Nobel Prize in Physiology and Medicine for his discovery of *Mycobacterium tuberculosis.*

1918: The worst flu outbreak in history, the Spanish flu, infects 20 to 40 percent of the world's population and kills at least 50 million people.

1921: French researchers Albert Calmette and Camille Guérin announce the creation of the BCG vaccine for TB.

1928: Scottish researcher Alexander Fleming discovers penicillin; it cures several deadly bacterial infections but not TB.

1939: The insecticide DDT is first used to control malaria during World War II.

1943: Streptomycin, the first effective antibiotic against TB, is discovered by American researchers Albert Schatz and Selman Waksman.

1946: Chloroquine is introduced to fight malaria.

c. 1947: Several strains of bacteria resistant to antibiotics appear worldwide; it remains a problem in developing areas.

1951: Malaria is eradicated as a major public health problem in the United States.

1952: Isoniazid is introduced for TB treatment.

1960s: Incidence of TB decreases worldwide, including in developing countries.

1961: First cases of methicillin-resistant *S. aureus* (MRSA) are discovered in British hospitals.

1970s: The number of TB cases starts rising around the world, especially in developing countries. The downward trend continues in the United States, where TB is thought to be eradicated.

1971: Rifampin is introduced for TB treatment.

1981: AIDS is first recognized in the United States.

1983: Doctors at the Pasteur Institute in France identify the retrovirus that causes AIDS.

1985: A blood test is developed to diagnose the AIDS virus, which is named the human immunodeficiency virus (HIV) in 1986. A TB epidemic occurs in New York City, and cases start rising again across the United States.

1993: The World Health Organization calls TB "a global emergency."

1996: Vancomycin-resistant *S. aureus* (VRSA) is identified in a Japanese hospital.

1996–2002: TB rates drop worldwide due to prevention and treatment programs.

1998: Rifapentine, first new TB drug in twenty-five years, becomes available. Genome of *Mycobacterium tuberculosis* is decoded.

2000: A drug-resistant strain of *Klebsiella pneumoniae* is found in a New York City hospital patient. A rash of similar deadly infections follows in other hospitals.

2001: The pneumococcal conjugate vaccine is introduced and given to children in the United States.

2008: The WHO reports that in some nations 20 percent of TB patients have drug-resistant strains.

2009: H1N1, a new flu virus, starts in Mexico in the early part of the year and spreads worldwide; a vaccine is available by the end of the year.

Chapter Notes

Introduction

1. Centers for Disease Control and Prevention, "Tuberculosis Data and Statistics," July 8, 2009, <http://www.cdc.gov/tb/statistics/default.htm> (July 17, 2009).
2. Centers for Disease Control and Prevention, "Malaria Facts," April 11, 2007, <http://www.cdc.gov/Malaria/facts.htm> (August 14, 2009).

Chapter 1: Understanding Tuberculosis

1. CNN, "Lawyer in 2007 TB Scare Sues CDC," April 30, 2009, <http://www.cnn.com/2009/CRIME/04/30/tb.lawsuit> (August 17, 2009); Lawrence K. Altman, "Reaction to TB Scare Gets Much Support," *The New York Times*, July 5, 2007, <http://www.nytimes.com/2007/07/05/health/05iht-health.4.6513832.html?_r=1> (July 28, 2009); Emerging Leaders in Public Health, "Crisis in the Sky: A Case Study in Miscommunication at the CDC," February 26, 2007, <http://www.publichealthleaders.org/curriculum/CrisisintheSky.ppsx> (August 23, 2009).
2. Centers for Disease Control and Prevention, "Tuberculosis Data and Statistics," July 8, 2009, <http://www.cdc.gov/tb/statistics/default.htm> (July 17, 2009).
3. Library Index, "Infectious Diseases: Tuberculosis," n.d., <http://www.libraryindex.com/pages/742/Infectious-Diseases-TUBERCULOSIS-TB.html> (July 21, 2009).
4. Mayo Clinic, "Tuberculosis: Causes," January 28, 2009, <http://www.mayoclinic.com/health/tuberculosis/DS00372/DSECTION=causes> (August 14, 2009).
5. eMedicine, "Tuberculosis," n.d., <http://emedicine.medscape.com/article/230802> (July 19, 2009).
6. Kenneth Todar, "*Mycobacterium tuberculosis* and Tuberculosis," *Todar's Online Textbook of Bacteriology*, 2009, <http://www.textbookofbacteriology.net/tuberculosis.html> (July 21, 2009).
7. National Agriculture Library, "Tuberculosis in Animals: Mycobacterium bacilli that cause Devastating Zoonotic Diseases in many Animals," December 2007, <http://www.nal.usda.gov/awic/pubs/TB/TBMain.htm> (August 14, 2009).
8. World Health Organization, "2008 Tuberculosis Facts," April 2008, <http://www.who.int/tb/publications/2008/factsheet_april08.pdf> (August 14, 2009).
9. Centers for Disease Control and Prevention, "Tuberculosis Data and Statistics."
10. eMedicine.
11. Mayo Clinic.
12. AVERT, "Worldwide HIV and AIDS Statistics," n.d.,<http://www.avert.org/worldstats.htm> (July 19, 2009).
13. Centers for Disease Control and Prevention, "TB and HIV/AIDS," January 2008, <http://www.cdc.gov/hiv/resources/factsheets/hivtb.htm> (August 14, 2009).

14. American Lung Association, "Lung Disease Data: 2008," 2008, <http://www.lungusa.org/assets/documents/publications/lung-disease-data/LDD_2008.pdf> (January 27, 2010).

15. World Health Organization.

16. Christopher Lettieri, "The Emergence and Impact of Extensively Drug-Resistant Tuberculosis," n.d., <http://www.medscape.com/viewarticle/557459_2> (August 14, 2009).

17. Stop TB Now, "What Is Tuberculosis?" n.d., <http://www.stoptbnow.com/tuberculosis.htm> (August 14, 2009).

18. Alliance Working for Antibiotic Resistance Education, "Antibiotic Facts," n.d., <http://www.aware.md/PatientsAndConsumers/AntibioticFacts.aspx> (August 14, 2009).

19. National Institutes of Health, "Fact Sheet: Tuberculosis," September 2007, <http://www.nih.gov/about/researchresultsforthepublic/Tuberculosis.pdf> (August 14, 2009).

20. Centers for Disease Control and Prevention, "Fact Sheet: Extensively Drug-Resistant Tuberculosis (XDR TB)," June 1, 2009, <http://www.cdc.gov/TB/publications/factsheets/drtb/xdrtb.htm> (August 14, 2009).

21. The Medical News, "The Focus on HIV/AIDS Has Helped Forget the Threat of Tuberculosis," March 25, 2008, <http://news-medical.net/news/2008/03/25/36649.aspx> (August 14, 2009).

22. National Public Radio, "How Common are Drug-Resistant Diseases?" June 1, 2007, <http://www.npr.org/templates/story/story.php?storyId=10613348> (July 20, 2009).

23. Orlando-Orange County Health Department, "TB's Famous Victims," n.d., <http://www.orchd.com/TB/FamousVictims.asp> (July 17, 2009); Tuberculosis and You, "Famous People Who Have Been Diagnosed and/or Died With Tuberculosis," n.d., <http://knowingabout.co.uk/tbandu/tbfamous.html> (July 17, 2009).

Chapter 2: Understanding Other Superbugs

1. Mayo Clinic, "MRSA Infection: Causes," May 30, 2008, <http://www.mayoclinic.com/health/mrsa/DS00735/DSECTION=causes> (July 24, 2009).

2. Centers for Disease Control and Prevention, "S. aureus and MRSA Surveillance Summary 2007," October 17, 2007, <http://www.cdc.gov/ncidod/dhqp/ar_mrsa_surveillanceFS.html> (August 4, 2009).

3. WebMD, "Understanding MRSA (Methicillin Resistant Staphylococcus Aureus)," December 1, 2008, <http://www.webmd.com/skin-problems-and-treatments/understanding-mrsa-methicillin-resistant-staphylococcus-aureus> (July 18, 2009).

4. Ibid.

5. Centers for Disease Control and Prevention, "Vancomycin-Resistant Staphylococcus aureus, Michigan, USA, 2007," June 25, 2009, <http://www.cdc.gov/EID/content/15/6/943.htm> (July 26, 2009).

6. Centers for Disease Control and Prevention, "Drug-Resistant Streptococcus pneumoniae," April 13, 2008, <http://www.cdc.gov/ncidod/dbmd/Diseaseinfo/drugresisstreppneum_t.htm> (July 25, 2009).

7. eMedicine, "Pneumococcal Infections," n.d., <http://emedicine.medscape.com/article/225811> (July 25, 2009).

8. Keep Antibiotics Working, "Factsheet: Antibiotic Resistance and Animal Agriculture," n.d., <http://keepantibioticsworking.com/new/resources_library.cfm?RefID=69872> (August 18, 2009).

9. David G. White et al., "The Isolation of Antibiotic-Resistant Salmonella from Retail Ground Meats," *New England Journal of Medicine*, October 18, 2001,<http://content.nejm.org/cgi/content/abstract/345/16/1147> (July 28, 2009).

10. Jerome Groopman, "Superbugs," *The New Yorker*, August 11, 2008, <http://www.newyorker.com/reporting/2008/08/11/080811fa_fact_groopman?currentPage=all> (August 18, 2009).

11. Ibid.

12. CNN, "Brazilian Amputee Model Dead at 20," January 24, 2009, <http://edition.cnn.com/2009/WORLD/americas/01/24/brazil.amputee.model/index.html> (August 17, 2009).

13. Centers for Disease Control and Prevention, "Malaria: Frequently Asked Questions," n.d., <http://www.cdc.gov/malaria/faq.htm> (July 25, 2009); Miguel C. Fernandez, MD, "Malaria," eMedicine, May 29, 2009, <http://emedicine.medscape.com/article/784065-overview>.

14. Ibid.

15. Centers for Disease Control and Prevention, "Malaria: Frequently Asked Questions."

16. Medical News Today, "Ivermectin Kills Head Lice Resistant to Standard Treatments," March 7, 2008, <http://www.medicalnewstoday.com/articles/99810.php> (July 27, 2009).

17. World Health Organization, "Frequently Asked Questions about TB and HIV," n.d., <http://www.who.int/tb/hiv/faq/en> (August 18, 2009).

18. Ibid.

19. Centers for Disease Control and Prevention, "HIV/AIDS in the United States," August 2009, <http://www.cdc.gov/hiv/resources/factsheets/us.htm> (August 18, 2009).

20. Planned Parenthood, "HIV/AIDS," n.d., <http://www.plannedparenthood.org/health-topics/stds-hiv-safer-sex/hiv-aids-4264.htm> (August 18, 2009).

21. Purdue University, "Research Leads to First Treatment for Drug-Resistant HIV," August 2, 2006, <http://www.chem.purdue.edu/NewsFeed/newsstory.asp?itemID=187> (July 27, 2009).

22. Centers for Disease Control and Prevention, "Seasonal Influenza: The Disease," August 11, 2009, <http://cdc.gov.flu/about/disease/> (August 18, 2009).

23. SINA English, "Death Toll of A/H1N1 Flu Rises, Study Finds New Flu Less Efficient Than Seasonal Flu," July 3, 2009 <http://english.sina.com/life/2009/0702/253033.html> (July 27, 2009).

Chapter 3: The History of TB and Other Superbugs

1. Kenneth Todar, "Mycobacterium tuberculosis and Tuberculosis," Todar's Online Textbook of Bacteriology, 2009, <http://www.textbookofbacteriology.net/tuberculosis.html> (February 24, 2010).

2. The Keats-Shelley House, "Tuberculosis," n.d., <http://www.keats-shelley-house.org/tuberculosis.php> (July 22, 2009).

3. Kenneth Kipple, *Plague, Pox, and Pestilence* (New York: Barnes and Noble Books, 1997), p. 136.

4. Nobelprize.org, "Robert Koch," n.d., <http://nobelprize.org/nobel_prizes/ medicine/laureates/1905/koch-bio.html> (July 28, 2009).

5. Lois Magner, *A History of Medicine* (Boca Raton, Fla.: Taylor & Francis, 2005), 2nd ed., p. 521.

6. Mark Caldwell, *The Last Crusade: The War of Consumption, 1862–1954* (New York: Athenaeum, 1988), p. 10.

7. Charlotte Williams, *Heroes of Health* (Chicago: Hall and McCleary, 1934), p. 86.

8. Erica Westly, "No Nobel for You: Top 10 Nobel Snubs," *Scientific American,* October 6, 2008, <http://www.scientificamerican.com/article.cfm?id=10-nobel-snubs> (November 3, 2009).

9. Peter D.O. Davies, "Multi-Drug Resistant Tuberculosis," March 1999, <http://priory.com/cmol/TBMultid.htm> (July 29, 2009).

10. Ibid.

11. Veronique Mistiaen, "Time, and the Great Healer," *The Guardian,* November 2, 2002, <http:www.guardian.co.uk/education/2002/nov/02/research. highereducation> (July 28, 2009).

12. Alison Bickford, "Twin Epidemics of Multidrug-Resistant Tuberculosis: Russia and New York City," *Virtual Mentor,* Vol. 8, No. 4, April 2006, <http://virtual-mentor.ama-assn.org/2006/04/msoc2-0604.html> (July 28, 2009).

13. W.F. Paolo, Jr., and J.D. Nosanchuk, "Tuberculosis in New York City: Recent Lessons and a Look Ahead," *Lancet Infectious Diseases,* May 2004, <http://www.ncbi.nlm.nih.gov/pubmed/15120345> (July 28, 2009).

14. TB Alliance, "Drug-Resistant TB," n.d., <http://www.tballiance.org/why/ mdr-tb.php> (July 28, 2009).

15. Bickford, "Twin Epidemics."

16. TB Alliance, "Drug-Resistant TB."

17. World Health Organization, "Global Tuberculosis Control – Surveillance, Planning, Financing," 2008, <http://www.who.int/tb/publications/global_ report/2008/summary/en/index.html> (August 18, 2009).

18. eMRSAfacts.com, "History of MRSA Infection," n.d., <http://www.emrsafacts. com/index.php/history-of-mrsa-infection> (July 29, 2009).

19. Centers for Disease Control, "Hospital Infections Cost U.S. Billions of Dollars Annually," March 6, 2000, <http://www.cdc.gov/media/pressrel/r2k0306b.htm> (August 18, 2009).

20. Jerome Groopman, "Superbugs," *The New Yorker,* August 11, 2008, <http://www.newyorker.com/reporting/2008/08/11fa_fact_groopman? currentPage=all> (August 18, 2009).

21. Ibid.

22. Centers for Disease Control and Prevention, "The History of Malaria, an Ancient Disease," April 23, 2004, <http://www.cdc.gov/malaria/history/index.htm> (July 29, 2009).

23. AIDS Education Global Information System, "So little time... An AIDS History," n.d., <http://www.aegis.com/topics/timeline/> (August 23, 2008).

24. AIDSOrigins, "Edward Hooper – A Brief Bio," May 25, 2004, <http://www. aidsorigins.com/content/view/23/30> (August 23, 2008).

25. U.S. Department of Health and Human Services, "Pandemics and Pandemic Threats Since 1900," <http://www.pandemicflu.gov/general/historicaloverview.html> n.d., (August 5, 2009).

26. GlobalSecurity.org, "1968 Hong Kong Flu," n.d., <http://www.globalsecurity.org/security/ops/hsc-scen-3_pandemic-1968.htm> (August 6, 2009).

27. SINA English, "Death Toll of A/H1N1flu rises, study finds new flu less efficient than seasonal flu," July 3, 2009, <http://english.sina.com/life/2009/0702/253033.html> (July 27, 2009).

Chapter 4: Preventing TB and Other Superbugs

1. The White House Office of the Press Secretary, "Statement by the President on Global Health Initiative," May 5, 2009, <http://www.whitehouse.gov/the_press_office/Statement-by-the-President-on-Global-Health-Initiative> (August 1, 2009).

2. World Health Organization, "Drug Resistance," n.d., <http://www.who.int/topics/drug_resistance/en/> (July 20, 2009).

3. TB Alert, "What is DOTS?" n.d., <http://www.tbalert.org/worldwide/DOTS.php> (August 8, 2009).

4. Ibid.

5. Centers for Disease Control and Prevention, "2009 H1N1 Flu ("Swine Flu") and You," July 15, 2009, <http://www.cdc.gov/H1N1flu/qa.htm> (July 27, 2009).

6. Edmund Sass, "The History of Polio," *The Polio History Pages*, January 21, 2006, <http://www.cloudnet.com/~edrbsass/poliotimeline.htm> (August 2, 2009).

7. C. Fordham von Reyn, "BCG Vaccination," *UpToDate*, August 15, 2002, <http://www.uptodate.com/patients/content/abstract.do?topicKey=~XDEX1uGLK2qGQT&refNum=1> (August 2, 2009).

8. Peter D. O. Davies, "Frequently Asked Questions about BCG," *Chest Medicine On-Line* <http://priory.com/cmol/bcg.htm> (August 18, 2009).

9. Immunization Action Coalition, "Pneumococcal Disease Questions & Answers," April 2009, <http://www.vaccineinformation.org/pneumchild/qandadis.asp> (November 5, 2009).

10. Centers for Disease Control and Prevention, "Drug-Resistant *Streptococcus pneumoniae Disease*," April 13, 2008 <http://www.cdc.gov/ncidod/DBMD/diseaseinfo/drugresisstreppneum_t.htm> (July 25, 2009).

11. eMedicine, "Pneumococcal Infections," n.d., <http://emedicine.medscape.com/article/225811-overview> (July 22, 2009).

12. American Society for Microbiology, "A Survey of Handwashing Behavior," September 2007, <http://www.cleaning101.com/newsroom/2007_survey/hand-hygiene/2007-(Trended)-Hand-Washing-Findings.ppt> (August 18, 2009).

13. Sarah Yang, "Smoking Increases Risk of TB Infection, Study Says," *PhysOrg*, February 27, 2007, <http://www.physorg.com/news91812761.html> (July 30, 2009).

14. Cedars-Sinai Medical Center, "Report to the Community 2008," 2008, <http://www.csmc.edu/pdf/2008AnnualReport-97522.pdf> (August 18, 2009).

15. Tessa Cunningham, "My son thought he'd never get malaria – so gave away the pills that would have saved him. But NO ONE is immune to this killer," *Mail Online*, June 11, 2009, <http://www.dailymail.co.uk/health/article-1191698/> (August 23, 2009).

Chapter 5: Testing and Treatment

1. Kenneth Kipple, *Plague, Pox, and Pestilence*, (New York: Barnes and Noble Books, 1997), p. 136.
2. North Carolina Department of Health and Human Services, "Instructions for Collecting Sputum for TB," n.d., <http://www.epi.state.nc.us/epi/tb/pdf/InstructionsforCollectingSputumforTB.pdf> (July 2, 2009).
3. M.F Brady et al., "The MODS Method for Diagnosis of Tuberculosis and Multidrug Resistant Tuberculosis," August 11, 2008, <http://www.ncbi.nlm.nih.gov/pubmed/19066507> (August 18, 2009).
4. Peter D.O. Davies, "Multi-Drug Resistant Tuberculosis," March 1999, <http://priory.com/cmol/TBMultid.htm> (July 29, 2009).
5. World Health Organization, "The Beijing 'Call for Action' on Tuberculosis Control and Patient Care," <http://www.who.int/tb_beijingmeeting/media/en_call_for_action.pdf> (August 1, 2009).
6. Henry J. Kaiser Family Foundation, "Drug-Resistant TB Can Spread As Easily as Drug-Sensitive TB, Study Says," *Medical News Today*, August 12, 2009, <http://www.MedicalNewsToday.com/articles/160463.php> (August 18, 2009).
7. Davies, "Multi-Drug Resistant Tuberculosis."
8. World Health Organization, "MDR-TB & XDR-TB The 2008 Report," February 26, 2008, <http://www.who.int/tb/features_archive/drsfactsheet.pdf> (August 18, 2009).
9. Gerald Friedland and Scott K. Heysell, "Epidemiology of Extensively Drug-Resistant Tuberculosis," *UpToDate*, n.d., <http://www.uptodate.com/patients/content/topic.do?topicKey=~sLsnLcrKCJ9hKTi> (August 8, 2009).
10. Medical News Today, "Extensively Drug-Resistant Tuberculosis (Xdr-Tb): The Facts," March 27, 2007 <http://www.medicalnewstoday.com/articles/66187.php> (August 10, 2009).
11. World Health Organization, "Key TB and TB/HIV Facts and Figures (World TB Day 2005)," n.d., <http://www.who.int/3by5/facts.pdf> (August 18, 2009).
12. UNAIDS, "MDR-TB More Common in People Living With HIV," February 28, 2008, <http://www.unaids.org/en/KnowledgeCentre/Resources/FeatureStories/archive/2008/20080227_MDR_rprt_for_UNAIDS.asp> (August 11, 2009).
13. Centers for Disease Control and Prevention, "National MRSA Education Initiative: Preventing MRSA Skin Infections," September 8, 2008, <http://www.cdc.gov/mrsa/mrsa_initiative/skin_infection/mrsa_hcp.html> (August 18, 2009).
14. WebMD, "Methicillin-Resistant *Staphylococcus aureus* (MRSA)," March 18, 2009, <http://www.webmd.com/a-to-z-guides/methicillin-resistant-staphylococcus-aureus-mrsa-overview> (August 12, 2009).
15. Diane Cochran, "Location of major infection a mystery," *Billings Gazette*, July 29, 2009, <http://www.billingsgazette.com/news/local/article_f8f270e2-7ccd-11de-a5d9-001cc4c03286.html> (November 18, 2009).
16. Centers for Disease Control and Prevention, "Malaria: Drug Resistance," April 23, 2004, <http://www.cdc.gov/malaria/drug_resistance.htm> (July 27, 2009).
17. Michael Smith, "WHO: Drug Resistance Expected in H1N1 Pandemic," *MedPage Today*, July 7, 2009, <http://www.medpagetoday.com/Infectious Disease/SwineFlu/14994> (November 19, 2009).

Chapter 6: Outlook for the Future

1. U.S. Department of Energy Office of Science, Office of Biological and Environmental Research, "Fun Facts about Microbes," September 23, 2005, <http://microbialgenomics.energy.gov/funfacts.shtml.> (August 14, 2009).
2. Ibid.
3. National Institute of Allergy and Infectious Diseases, "The Whole Ball of Wax: TB's Distinctive Cell Wall," April 1, 2005, <http:www3.niaid.nih.gov/topics/tuberculosis/Research/basicResearch/biology_cell.htm> (August 14, 2009).
4. Amy Adams, "Genetics 101: Overview of Genetics," *Genetic Health*, November 19, 2000, <http://www.genetichealth.com/G101_Genetics_Demystified.shtml> (August 17, 2009).
5. Ibid.
6. H.I. Boshoff and C.E. Barry III, "A low-carb diet for a high-octane pathogen," *Nature Medicine*, Vol. 11, 2005, pp. 599–600.
7. National Institute of Allergy and Infectious Diseases, "How Mycobacteria Make Themselves at Home," March 30, 2005, <http://www3.niaid.nih.gov/topics/tuberculosis/Research/basicResearch/about_mycobacteria> (August 15, 2009).
8. Ernesto J. Muñoz-Elías and John D. McKinney, "Mycobacterium tuberculosis isocitrate lyases 1 and 2 are jointly required for in vivo growth and virulence," *Nature Medicine*, Vol., 11, 2005, pp. 638–644.
9. Science Daily, "One Secret to How TB Sticks With You," July 13, 2009, <http://www.sciencedaily.com/releases/2009/07/09070912741.htm> (July 23, 2009).
10. EurekAlert!, "Tuberculosis Drugs Under Development Expected to Have Major Impact on the Disease," August 3, 2009, <http://www.eurekalert.org/pub_releases/2009-08/fhcr-tdu072909.php> (August 15, 2009).
11. Vanderbilt University, "Study of Ineffective TB Vaccine May Lead to New Vaccines," May 21, 2009, <http://sitemason.vanderbilt.edu/myvu/news/2009/05/21/study-of-ineffective-tb-vaccine-may-lead-to-new-vaccines.80590> (August 15, 2009)
12. Ibid.
13. IRIN, "Global: When Every Day Is TB Day," March 25, 2009, <http://irin-news.org/Report.aspx?ReportId=83637%20> (August 15, 2009).
14. TB Alliance, "TB Alliance and Tibotec Chart Innovative Development Paradigm for TB Drugs," July 2009, <http://www.tballiance.org/newscenter/newsletters/jul09/newsletter-jul09.html> (August 16, 2009).
15. Science Daily, "Existing Parkinson's Disease Drug May Fight Drug-Resistant TB," July 4, 2009, <http://www.sciencedaily.com/releases/2009/07/090703065218.htm> (July 20, 2009).
16. National Institute of Allergy and Infectious Diseases, "New Ammunition against an Old Enemy: Multiple Approaches to TB Therapy," March 20, 2006, <http:www3.niaid.nih.gov/topics/tuberculosis/Research/treatment/twoApproaches.htm> (August 16, 2009).
17. National Institute of Allergy and Infectious Diseases, "A Timely Test: All-in-One Cartridge May Speed TB Detection," March 24, 2009, <http://www3.niaid.nih.gov/topics/tuberculosis/Research/diagnostic/diagnosis_test.htm> (August 16, 2009); Cepheid, "Xpert MTB/RIF," n.d., <http://www.cepheid.com/media/files/eu/brochures/XpertMTB_Broch_R9_EU.pdf> (August 16, 2009).

18. Censorbugbear, "Rats to Detect Tuberculosis in South Africa," <http://censorbug-bear-reports.blogspot.com/2009/06/rats-to-detect-tuberculosis-in-south.html> (August 15, 2009); Colin Nickerson, "Mankind's New Best Friend," *The Boston Globe*, November 23, 2008, <http://www.boston.com/news/science/articles/2008/11/23/mankinds_new_best_friend> (August 8, 2009); Wendell Roelf, "South Africa leads hunt for killer TB vaccine," Reuters, June 4, 2009, <http://www.satvi.uct.ac.za/news/south-africa-leads-hunt-for-killer-tb-vaccine.html> (February 10, 2010).

19. Rapid Biosensor Systems, "Tackling the Worldwide TB Epidemic," n.d., <http://www.rapidbiosensor.com/tb_breathalyser.asp> (August 16, 2009).

20. Sequella, "Product Summaries: TB Patch Diagnostic," n.d., <http://sequella.com/pipeline/product_summaries.xhtml> (August 17, 2009).

21. Foundation for Innovative New Diagnostics, June 27, 2008, <http://www.find-diagnostics.org/export/sites/default/media/news/pdf/lpa_policy_statement.pdf> (August 14, 2007).

22. Centers for Disease Control and Prevention, "Prevalence of *S. aureus* and MRSA Colonization," October 17, 2007, <http://www.cdc.gov/ncidod/dhqp/ar_mrsa_sur-veillanceFS.html> (August 4, 2009).

23. *The Economist*, "The Way a Superbug Tries to Survive Might Provide a Treatment," June 11, 2009, <http://www.economist.com/sciencetechnology/displayStory.cfm?Story_id=13815133> (August 13, 2009).

24. American Institute of Physics, "Pathologists Invent Easy Way to Diagnose MRSA," August 1, 2007, <http://aip.org/dbis/stories/2007/17085.html> August 17, 2009).

25. Bob Roehr, "5-Hour Diagnostic Test for MRSA," *Medscape*, October 26, 2008, <http://www.medscape.com/viewarticle/582588> (August 11, 2009).

26. Bio-Medicine, "NOW Streptococcus Test," n.d., <http://www.bio-medicine.org/medicine-products/NOW-26reg-3B-Streptococcus-pneumoniae> (August 16, 2009).

27. Spotlight on Prevention, "Antibiotic-Coated Medical Devices Could Cut Infections," January 19, 2007, <http://hospitalacquiredinfections.blogspot.com/search/lavel/Antibiotic-Coated%20Medical-Devices-Could-Cut-Infections> (August 1, 2009).

28. HospiMedica, "Copper Fixtures Kill Most Hospital Microbes," November 10, 2008, <http://www.hospimedica.com/?option=com_article&Itemid=294720982&cat=Patient Care> (August 16, 2009).

29. EurekAlert! "New Lead on Malaria Treatment," May 18, 2009, <http://eurekalert.org/pub_releases/2009-05/jhmi-nlo051809.php> (July 27, 2009).

30. America.gov, "Immune Response Stops Malaria Parasite Development," March 16, 2009, <http://www.america.gov/st/develop-english/2009/March/20090316141332lcnirellep0.0395624.html> (August 17, 2009).

31. Free Press News Services, "Malaria: Scientists Ready to Start Human Tests on Vaccine," *Detroit Free Press*, July 27, 2009, <http://pqasb.pqarchiver.com/freep/access/1803857721.html?dids=1803857721:1803857721&FMT=ABS&FMTS=ABS:FT&type=current&date=Jul+26%2C+2009&author=&pub=Detroit+Free+Press&edition=&startpage=A.32&desc=Medical+advances> (August 27, 2009).

32. International AIDS Vaccine Initiative, "Database of AIDS Vaccine Candidates in Clinical Trials," n.d., <http://www.iavireport.org/trials-db/Pages/TrialResults.aspx?TDBQuery=6e0c2466-f83c-4a7c-b16a-58b86ae00dc8> (August 17, 2009).

33. Kate Proctor, "Malaria: The Holiday Bug With a Lethal Sting," *The Independent*, July 7, 2009, <http://www.Independent.co.uk/life-style/health-and-families/features/malaria-the-holiday-bug-with-a-lethal-sting-1734271.html> (July 22, 2009).

34. Science Daily, "Fighting Drug-resistant Flu Viruses," July 16, 2009, <http://www.sciencedaily.com/releases/2009/07/090715101438.htm> (August 3, 2009).

Chapter 7: Living with TB and Other Superbugs

1. Medline Plus, "Infectious Diseases," May 8, 2009, <http://www.nlm.nih.gov/medlineplus/infectiousdiseases.html> (August 21, 2009).

2. Elizabeth Fernandez, "Study Finds a Different Type of TB Patient," *San Francisco Chronicle*, March 25, 2009, <http://www.sfgate.com/cgi-bin/article.cgi?f=/c/a/2009/03/24/BA8S16MBVA.DTL> (August 21, 2009).

3. UNAIDS, "Cartoons to Help Stop Tuberculosis," June 12, 2009, <http://www.unaids.org/en/KnowledgeCentre/Resources/FeatureStories/archive/2009/20090611_TB_Cartoons.asp> (August 23, 2009).

4. Elizabeth Chiles Shelburne, "Part I: The Deadly New Tuberculosis," *GlobalPost*, January 14, 2009, <http://www.globalpost.com/dispatch/health/090103/part-i-the-deadly-new-tuberculosis> (August 21, 2009).

5. Carole Bartoo, "New MRSA Form Harsher on Teens," *Reporter*, May 25, 2007, <http://www.mc.vanderbilt.edu/reporter/index.html?ID=5570> (August 17, 2009).

6. Tom Withers, "A Growing Threat: Staph Infections Rising Among Athletes," *The Monterey Herald*, November 23, 2006, <http://www.teclabsinc.com/press-detail.cfm?id=2AC23C53-A7AB-2A26-44EFEE1038BFCCDC> (August 21, 2009).

7. Mark Maske, "NFL Has Low Staph Rate, Report Says," *The Washington Post*, March 12, 2009, <http://views.washingtonpost.com/theleague/nflnewsfeed/2009/03/nfl-has-low-staph-rate-report-says.html> (August 21, 2009).

8. Brandon Noble, "Draft from Testimony Before the Senate Committee on Health, Education, Labor & Pensions," June 24, 2008," <http://www.help.senate.gov/Hearings/2008_06_24/Noble.pdf> (August 21, 2008).

9. Mark Maske and Jason La Canfora, "A Frightening Off-Field Foe," *The Washington Post*, January 27, 2006, <http://www.washingtonpost.com/wp-dyn/content/article/2006/01/26/AR2006012602171.html> (August 21, 2008).

10. Malaria Hotspots, "Protect against Malaria," n.d., <http://www.malaria-hotspots.co.uk/protectingYourself.asp> (August 21, 2008).

Glossary

active TB disease—The contagious form of TB, in which bacteria are multiplying, producing cough, fatigue, and other symptoms.

alveoli—Tiny air sacs inside the lungs where the exchange of oxygen and carbon dioxide takes place.

antibiotic—A drug used to treat bacterial infections.

antibodies—Proteins made by the body to protect itself from foreign substances, such as bacteria or viruses.

attenuated vaccine—A vaccine made of weakened live organisms, such as bacteria or viruses, or the proteins derived from them.

bacilli—Rod-shaped, usually gram-positive bacteria, such as the ones that cause *M. tuberculosis*.

Bacillus Calmette-Guérin (BCG)—A TB vaccine developed in the 1920s and still widely used in countries other than the United States.

bacteria—Single-celled microorganisms that need oxygen to live and grow. Only one percent are harmful.

bovine TB—Another name for *M. bovis*, a type of TB found in mammals, especially cattle, deer, bison, and goats, but rarely in humans.

Centers for Disease Control and Prevention (CDC)—A U.S. government agency that tracks, prevents, and controls chronic and infectious diseases and educates the public about them.

consumption—An early name for TB that described how the disease seemed to consume the body.

culture—A laboratory test of tissue or body fluids to see which microorganisms are responsible for infections. Results can take two to four weeks.

Directly Observed Treatment, Short-course (DOTS)—A protocol that helps TB patients take their medicine correctly by having people monitor their treatment.

drug resistance—The ability of a microorganism to resist an antibiotic or other drug that was once able to obstruct or destroy it.

extensively drug-resistant TB (XDR-TB)—TB disease caused by a strain of bacteria resistant to most antibiotics used to treat it.

extrapulmonary TB—TB disease in any part of the body other than the lungs (for example, the kidneys or lymph nodes).

false negative—An imperfect test result that says what is looked for is not there when it actually is.

false positive—An imperfect test result that says what is looked for is there when it actually is not.

Gram stain—A way of staining bacteria to identify and classify them under a microscope.

immune system—A complex system, made up of organs and cells, which protects the body from infections, diseases, and foreign substances through a process called the immune response.

latent TB infection—A noncontagious condition in which TB bacteria are alive but inactive in the body.

macrophage—A white blood cell that ingests foreign substances and is a key player in the immune response.

Mantoux test—A skin test used to diagnose TB infection.

methicillin-resistant *Staphylococcus aureus* (MRSA)—A potentially fatal bacterial infection resistant to the antibiotics usually used to treat staph.

microorganism—A microscopic organism, like a bacterium or parasite; also called a microbe.

miliary TB—TB disease that has spread to the whole body through the bloodstream.

multidrug-resistant TB (MDR-TB)—TB disease caused by a strain of bacteria resistant to more than one drug commonly used to treat it.

mutation—A change in the gene structure that is passed on to offspring. The genes of microorganisms that cause infectious diseases can mutate, pass these traits on to other microorganisms, and eventually become resistant to many drugs.

Mycobacterium tuberculosis—The bacterium that causes latent TB and active TB disease.

nosocomial infection—An infection that is acquired in a hospital, nursing home, or residential health-care setting.

pneumococcal conjugate vaccine—A vaccine given to children and adults to prevent pneumococcal disease, including pneumonia and meningitis.

prime boosting—A vaccination technique in which an initial shot is followed later by a booster shot to increase protection.

pulmonary TB—TB disease that occurs in the lungs; the most common type of TB.

sputum—The material, also called phlegm, coughed up from deep in the lungs. Sputum samples are collected and tested for TB bacteria.

superbug—A disease-causing microorganism that becomes resistant to drugs normally used to kill or control it.

tubercle—A small, firm nodule characteristically found in the lungs of TB patients.

tuberculin—The TB protein injected under the skin during the Mantoux test.

vaccine—Killed or weakened microorganisms used to prevent disease by stimulating the immune system; usually given by injection and occasionally by nasal spray.

virus—A microorganism, smaller than a bacterium, that needs a living cell in order to grow or reproduce.

For More Information

Further Reading

Allman, Toney. *Tuberculosis*. San Diego, Calif.: Lucent Books, 2006.

Fandel, Jennifer. *Louis Pasteur and Pasteurization*. Mankato, Minn.: Capstone Press, 2007.

Farrell, Jeanette. *Invisible Allies: Microbes That Shape Our Lives*. New York: Farrar, Straus, and Giroux, 2005.

———. *Invisible Enemies: Stories of Infectious Diseases*. New York: Farrar, Straus, Giroux, 2005.

Marrin, Albert. *Oh, Rats!: The Story of Rats and People*. New York: Dutton Children's Books, 2006.

Tracy, Kathleen. *Robert Koch and the Study of Anthrax*. Hockessin, DE: Mitchell Lane Publishers, 2004.

Yancey, Diane. *Tuberculosis*. Minneapolis: Twenty-First Century Books, 2008.

Internet Addresses

Medline Plus: Tuberculosis.
    <http://www.nlm.nih.gov/medlineplus/tuberculosis.html>

Stop TB Partnership.
    <http://www.stoptb.org/>

Organizations

Centers for Disease Control and Prevention (CDC)
Division of Tuberculosis Elimination
1600 Clifton Road, NE
Atlanta, GA 30333
(404) 639-3534
Toll free: 1-800-311-3435
<http://www.cdc.gov/nchstp/tb/>

Centers for Disease Control and Prevention (CDC)
National Prevention Information Network
P.O. Box 6003
Rockville, MD 20849-6003
(800) 458-5231
<http://www.cdcnpin.org/scripts/index.asp>

Keep Antibiotics Working
P.O. Box 14590
Chicago, IL 60614
(773) 525-4952
<http://www.keepantibioticsworking.com>

TB Alliance
40 Wall Street, 24th Floor
New York, NY 10005
(212) 227-7540
<http://www.tballiance.org>

World Health Organization
Avenue Appia 20
1211 Geneva 27
Switzerland
+41 22 791 21 11
<http:/www.who.int/en/>

Index